The Navajo

Indigenous Peoples of North America

The Navajo

Patricia Cronin Marcello

Lucent Books, Inc.
P.O. Box 289011, San Diego, California

Titles in the Indigenous Peoples of North America Series Include:

The Apache

The Cherokee

The Iroquois

Native Americans of the Great Lakes

Native Americans of the Northeast

Native Americans of the Plains

Native Americans of the Southeast

Native Americans of the Southwest

The Navajo

The Sioux

Library of Congress Cataloging-in-Publication Data

Marcello, Patricia Cronin.
    The Navajo / by Patricia Cronin Marcello.
        p.   cm. — (Indigenous peoples series)
    Includes bibliographical references and index.
    ISBN 1-56006-619-9

Contents

Foreword

North America's native peoples are often relegated to history—viewed primarily as remnants of another era—or cast in the stereotypical images long found in popular entertainment and even literature. Efforts to characterize Native Americans typically result in idealized portrayals of spiritualists communing with nature or bigoted descriptions of savages incapable of living in civilized society. Lost in these unfortunate images is the rich variety of customs, beliefs, and values that comprised—and still comprise—many of North America's native populations.

The *Indigenous Peoples of North America* series strives to present a complex, realistic picture of the many and varied Native American cultures. Each book in the series offers historical perspectives as well as a view of contemporary life of individual tribes and tribes that share a common region. The series examines traditional family life, spirituality, interaction with other native and non-native peoples, warfare, and the ways the environment shaped the lives and cultures of North America's indigenous populations. Each book ends with a discussion of life today for the Native Americans of a given region or tribe.

In any discussion of the Native American experience, there are bound to be sim-

ilarities. All tribes share a past filled with unceasing white expansion and resistance that led to more than four hundred years of conflict. One U.S. administration after another pursued this goal and fought Indians who attempted to defend their homelands and ways of life. Although no war was ever formally declared, the U.S. policy of conquest precluded any chance of white and Native American peoples living together peacefully. Between 1780 and 1890, Americans killed hundreds of thousands of Indians and wiped out whole tribes.

The Indians lost the fight for their land and ways of life, though not for lack of bravery, skill, or a sense of purpose. They simply could not contend with the overwhelming numbers of whites arriving from Europe or the superior weapons they brought with them. Lack of unity also contributed to the defeat of the Native Americans. For most, tribal identity was more important than racial identity. This loyalty left the Indians at a distinct disadvantage. Whites had a strong racial identity and they fought alongside each other even when there was disagreement because they shared a racial destiny.

Although all Native Americans share this tragic history they have many distinct differences. For example, some tribes and individuals sought to cooperate almost immediately with the U.S. government while others steadfastly resisted the white presence. Life before the arrival of white settlers also varied. The nomads of the Plains developed altogether different lifestyles and customs from the fishermen of the Northwest coast.

Contemporary life is no different in this regard. Many Native Americans—forced onto reservations by the American government—struggle with poverty, poor health, and inferior schooling. But others have regained a sense of pride in themselves and their heritage, enabling them to search out new routes to self-sufficiency and prosperity.

The *Indigenous Peoples of North America* series attempts to capture the differences as well as similarities that make up the experiences of North America's native populations—both past and present. Fully documented primary and secondary source quotations enliven the text. Sidebars highlight events, personalities, and traditions. Bibliographies provide readers with ideas for further research. In all, each book in this dynamic series provides students with a wealth of information as well as launching points for further research.

The People of Dinetah

The southwestern United States is famous for its many physical wonders. Picturesque settings like the Grand Canyon, the Petrified Forest, and Monument Valley are unique in the world. Yet more fascinating than the enchanting land are the people who live there.

Many different indigenous peoples, including the Paiute, the Zuni, the Apache, the Havasupai, the Yavapai, the Pima, the Maricopa, the Papago, the Tewa, and the Hopi, live and work in the area. Some of these tribes are referred to as Pueblo Indians, a name derived from their custom of living in apartment-style adobe dwellings. From them, the Navajo people learned valuable ways to survive in the harsh desert climate.

This ability has helped the Navajo to remain a powerful nation today. With a total population of over two hundred thousand people, the Navajo Nation is now the largest tribe in the Southwest. Most of its members live on a reservation, a special portion of land that the U.S. government set aside for them in 1868. The Navajo call this land Dinetah or Navajoland. It rests in a portion of three states—Arizona, New Mexico, and Utah—and has a total area about the same size as the state of West Virginia (twenty-five thousand square miles). Navajoland is the largest Native American reservation in the country.

Parts of the reservation resemble other small cities in the United States. Fast-food restaurants, shopping malls, and supermarkets cater to tourists and local residents alike. Other parts of the reservation, where only trading posts serve local customers, resemble rural small towns. Large portions of the reservation are still wild and remote.

In many of the out-of-the-way locations, tribe members depend on shepherding and farming for their survival, as they have done for centuries. In another long-standing activity, many Navajo earn money making jewelry, rugs, and other traditional crafts. Modern-day big business has also come to parts of the reservation in the form of mining and power generation. Besides creating income for the tribe, these industries provide work for some Navajo people. However, few regular, full-time jobs are available, and many Navajo must leave the reservation to find suitable work.

Most Navajo, however, prefer to live on the reservation, where they feel at home with their own people. Here, they have formed a well-respected, organized body of self-governance. While outside industries continue to provide income, the tribe makes plans for Navajo-owned and -operated businesses in the future. Most remarkably, as the modern world hums around them, the Navajo have remained true to their ancient culture.

Their story is one of defeat and triumph, heartache and joy. It is a story of balance, which the Navajo strive to achieve in all that they do. A Navajo prayer, reprinted on the Spirit of Beauty website, expresses the pride of the Navajo people who, like their ancestors, strive to "walk in beauty."

In beauty may I walk.
All day long may I walk.
Through the returning seasons
    may I walk.
On the trail marked with pollen
    may I walk.
With grasshoppers about my feet
    may I walk.

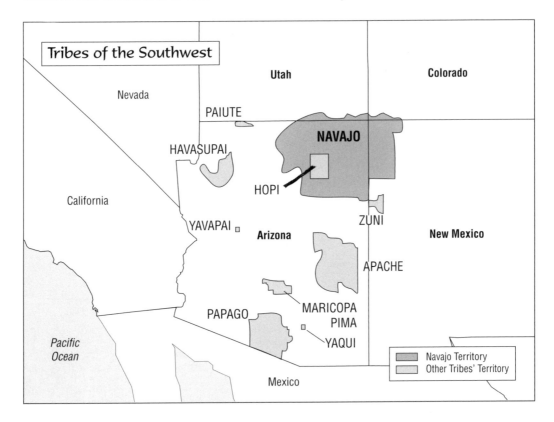

Tribes of the Southwest

Nevada

Utah

Colorado

PAIUTE

HAVASUPAI

NAVAJO

HOPI

California

YAVAPAI

Arizona

ZUNI

New Mexico

APACHE

PAPAGO

MARICOPA
PIMA

Pacific
Ocean

YAQUI

Navajo Territory
Other Tribes' Territory

Mexico

With dew about my feet may I walk.
With beauty may I walk.
With beauty before me, may I walk.
With beauty behind me, may I walk.
With beauty above me, may I walk.
With beauty below me, may I walk.

In old age wandering on a trail of
    beauty, lively, may I walk.
In old age wandering on a trail of
    beauty, living again, may I walk.
It is finished in beauty.
It is finished in beauty.[1]

Chapter 1

Coming to Four Corners

The area where Colorado, Utah, New Mexico, and Arizona meet is fittingly called Four Corners. Here, more than five hundred years ago, a group of nomadic hunting people from northwest North America chose to make their home. They call themselves the Dine', which means "the People"; others know them as the Navajo Nation.

Three thousand years ago the Israelites were choosing David as their king. At about that same time, a group of Asian people crossed into the territory now called Alaska. Scholars believe that they traveled across a land bridge that once existed across the Bering Strait. Why they came into North America is not certain; however, their lifestyle of following the herds of animals they hunted for food suggests that they were in search of new sources of game.

These scouts were the Na-dene, and they spoke a common language. They were strong and adapted easily to new territories and situations. With their dark hair, angular faces, and thin lips, the Na-dene resembled the Mongolian people who continue to live in Asia today.

Jesus was born two thousand years ago. Around that same time, the Na-Dene split into two groups. One group became the Tlingit and the Haida tribes of the northwestern coast of North America. The other group came to be known as the Athabascans (or Athapaskans). They gathered in loosely organized groups in Alaska and near Lake Athabasca, which stretches across northern Alberta and Saskatchewan in Canada.

Around the first millennium, one thousand years ago, Leif Eriksson made his voyage to North America. On the opposite side of the continent, some Athabascans began traveling southward. They followed wild game (like deer and caribou), they fished, and less often, they foraged for wild nuts and berries. Because they were constantly moving, permanent dwellings did not suit their needs, so they constructed temporary tents by draping

The Glittering World

According to traditional Dine' beliefs, the present world, which exists on the surface of the earth, was preceded by three other worlds. The Dine' say that this is the Fourth, or Glittering, World, and stories of how this came about are sacred to the Navajo people. Although the events described in the stories are fantastic by modern standards, the stories convey an important message.

The Navajo basic creation story is complicated, with many characters, places, and events. First there was the Black World, where First Man and First Woman were created. But the creatures here could not get along, so they moved upward through a hole in the sky into Second, or Blue, World. Yet it was dry and cheerless, so the beings and creatures continued to move upward into Yellow, or Third, World, where monsters created a great flood. To escape it, all of the people and creatures in Yellow World climbed through a reed that grew into the sky. They emerged in the present, known as the Glittering World.

Storytellers tend to add or subtract parts of the story, depending on how they learned the story, how much time they have to tell it, or any number of different reasons. Thus, many versions exist: In some versions there are four worlds; in others there are five. In *FAQs About Life on the Navajo Nation and Among the Navajo People*, edited by Larry DiLucchio, a Navajo medicine man explains why there are so many versions: "Too many Story Tellers!"

The Journey South

Most of what is known about the Athabascans has been deduced from years of scientific study. "It is difficult to know what Athabascan culture was in this period of southern migration or even what the route of the movement was,"[2] writes anthropologist James F. Downs in *The Navajo*.

Yet experts believe that the Athabascans kept moving. They arrived in northern Arizona and New Mexico some five hundred years ago, around the time that William Shakespeare wrote *Romeo and Juliet*. Although the exact time of their arrival remains in question, the migration probably happened over many generations, and the people probably trickled down from Canada in clusters rather than as a whole group. "But even without archaeological support, we can safely assume that the Athabascans did come into the southwest and there they developed a number of separate but related cultures and languages,"[3] Downs writes.

These people came wearing buckskin clothing and carried few material possessions. They were no doubt surprised when they discovered the Pueblo tribes, who had already been in the area for about nine hundred years. animal skins over a central wooden pole. They were not a highly skilled people, and their only arts were making strong baskets and undecorated, serviceable pottery.

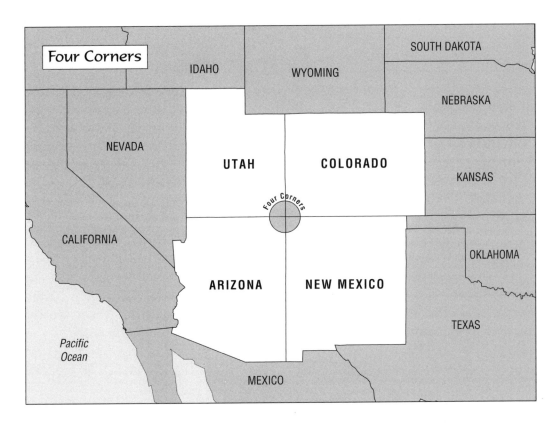

Meeting the Prosperous Neighbors

Although the Pueblo tribes are related, they are not one nation. The Hopi, the Acoma, the Zuni, and the Laguna are a few tribes, but there are many different pueblos, or Native American villages, in the Four Corners area. The discovery of so many different towns extending from Arizona to New Mexico may be one reason why the Athabascan travelers decided to stay in this region.

Centuries before the Athabascans arrived, the Pueblo Indians had learned how to grow crops in the arid desert. Their permanent adobe dwellings made them seem very rich and ripe for plunder. The Athabascans found it easier to survive by regularly raiding the many different pueblos rather than by searching for food and water in the arid desert region.

Eventually some Athabascans took more than possessions from the Pueblo tribes—they learned some Pueblo ways. They discarded their buckskin clothing for lighter fabrics such as cotton, which was better suited to the desert climate. The Athabascans also learned to raise crops like beans, squash, corn, and tobacco. This group settled in the northern Arizona-New Mexico and southern Utah-Colorado regions to take up farming. Another group continued their life of nomadic hunting and gathering, moving farther south. The group that learned farming became the Navajo tribe; the other group became the Apache. Although scientists generally agree on this account, it is only an educated guess; no physical evidence exists to prove that this is actually what happened.

Father Alonzo de Benavides, a Spanish missionary, first wrote about the separation of the Athabascans in 1630. He named one group the Apaches de Nabajo, which probably meant "large cultivated fields," and suggested their farming skills. He called the other group the Vaquero (meaning "cowboy") Apache, which most likely indicated that they hunted buffalo.

This description by a contemporary observer is another indication that the two tribes were related.

Roots of Navajo Tradition

Traditional Navajo beliefs do not include a journey across the Bering Strait or a sojourn among the Pueblo Indians. The ancestral teachings, instead, refer to certain Yei, or "Holy Ones," the tribe's spiritual guides, who are said to have told the Dine' to make their home among four mountains. The San Francisco Peaks in Arizona represent their western boundary, Blanca Peak in Colorado represents their eastern boundary, Mount Taylor in New Mexico represents their southern boundary, and

The Formidable Apache

Although the Navajo and the Apache have common ancestors, the tribes went their separate ways sometime before the seventeenth century. The Navajo settled down to become farmers and built semipermanent houses. The Apache continued wandering the land in search of food. They lived in tepees (cone-shaped tents framed with saplings and covered with animal skins) or wickiups (dome-shaped huts framed with saplings and covered by brush or brush mats). Both dwellings were easily put up and taken down.

Eventually the Mescalero and the Jicarilla Apache settled in New Mexico. Other Apache tribespeople moved into Arizona and became the White Mountain and the Chiricahua Apaches, but there are many other Apache groups in the Four Corners region. There are also some Apache bands stretching into Oklahoma, including the Kiowa Apache.

Historically, the Apache have exhibited an impressive level of physical fitness. Living off the land was second nature, and their endurance was legendary: These fierce warriors could go naked in temperatures well below freezing, if the need arose. They could also travel vast distances on foot with very little water. They were respected and feared throughout the Southwest.

A Navajo hut in Monument Valley, part of the Navajo reservation that contains some of the most beautiful landscape in the world.

Hesperus Peak, also in Colorado, represents the tribe's northern boundary. The Dine' say that the Holy Ones told them that if they lived within these limits, they would always be protected.

"Our offering places are sacred to us, and the spiritual beings take care of us. We know the land; the spiritual beings know us here. If we leave our offering places, we will not be able to survive,"[4] says Jack Hatathlie, a Navajo medicine man.

The land within these mountain boundaries once identified Navajo territory. Today, the Navajo reservation, as defined by the U.S. government, is somewhat smaller in area. Still, Navajoland contains some of the most magnificent landscape in the world.

Wandering Through Monument Valley

One sacred spot in Navajoland is Monument Valley. Here, towering spires of sandstone rock and chunky red buttes rise up from the flat desert valley. Many of them are familiar to people who have never been in the valley before. Several commercials have been made in Monument Valley, and it has been the backdrop for many western movies. Yet the land is holy to the Navajo, who say that "the gods use the valley's mesa tops as steppingstones when they walk the Earth."[5]

The Valley of the Standing Rocks. The Navajo believe that the gods use these mesas as stepping stones when they come to earth.

An ocean once existed where Monument Valley sits, but that was more than 25 million years ago. Weather, including wind, rain, and temperature fluctuations, caused erosion of the hardened sediment deposits. The buttes, spires, and desert sand are what remain. Some of the names of the buttes and spires include Right Mitten, Left Mitten, the King on His Throne, Bear and Rabbit, Three Sisters, Elephant Butte, and Eagle Mesa. "We just called it the Valley of the Standing Rocks,"[6] says Navajo Donald Fatt.

Canyon de Chelly as Home to the Navajo

In central Navajoland is Canyon de Chelly, where humans have lived since 2500 B.C. Here, the more than 200-million-year-old walls of red, russet, and brown sandstone range from thirty feet to almost one thousand feet high. Although Canyon de Chelly is the largest canyon in the area, other connecting canyons include Canyon del Muerto, Monument Canyon, and Black Rock Canyon, which is much smaller than the other three.

Canyon de Chelly was once home to the Pueblo ancestors known as the Anasazi, although the Pueblo tribes prefer to call them the Hisatsinom. No one knows the real name of the people who once lived here. The name *Anasazi* is a Navajo word meaning "Enemy Ancestor."

The Anasazi built their homes in cliffs overlooking the canyons. In addition to being dedicated farmers and creative craftspeople who made pottery, baskets, and jewelry, the Anasazi appear to have been sophisticated astronomers who tracked the position of the sun from rock-hewn observatories. But they left the canyon by about A.D. 1300. "The Anasazi abandoned their homeland, leaving the great stone cities and familiar farmlands for other areas of the Southwest,"[7] writes Donald G. Pike in his book *Anasazi: Ancient People of the Rock*.

The reason they abandoned their well-ordered society is still a mystery. Some say a terrible drought forced the ancient culture

Navajo Myths: The Creation and Salvation of the Dine'

In the Glittering World, the four sacred mountains were created, the stars arose in the sky, and the sun and moon were formed. The seasons were set, day and night were divided, and the first crops were grown and harvested. But all went wrong when monsters arrived and began killing people. It took a miracle to save them.

Atop a mountain, First Man and First Woman found a baby, whom they named Changing Woman. She matured quickly, and a ceremony was held in honor of her new adult status. Sometime afterward, Changing Woman fell asleep by a waterfall, and the sun came to her. They united, and the hero twins Child Born of Water and Monster Slayer were born.

While the twins were growing, Changing Woman mixed cornmeal with her own skin scrapings and formed the Navajo people. However, the land was not safe for the Navajo because the monsters were still roaming the land; they needed the hero twins to save them.

Child Born of Water and Monster Slayer met Spider Woman. She told them who their father was, but instead of immediately acknowledging his sons, the sun put them through many horrible trials. Strong and powerful in their own right, the twins met and mastered the tasks. Their father then accepted them and gave them lightning bolts with which to fight. Child Born of Water and Monster Slayer managed to kill all of the monsters, except the ones that caused old age, lice, hunger, and death. The dead monsters are still present, however, for it is believed that they turned to stone as they fell. Thus, all of the striking rock formations on the reservation are seen as petrified monsters.

to leave to find water. Others suspect that rival tribes had raided them too often. Some say one of the raiding tribes was the Navajo; possibly, the raiders were Athabascans from an early migration. Regardless of why the Anasazi left, the Navajo benefited as the canyon eventually became theirs; however, they probably did not take it over completely until about 1700.

In Canyon de Chelly, the Navajo found not only ruins of a once-flourishing society but also the Rio de Chelly, a river that twisted its way through the canyon's bottom. Its water supported cottonwood and tamarisk trees. Coyotes, bobcats, beavers, raccoons, wild turkeys, cottontail rabbits, pack rats, mice, and porcupines lived in the canyon while ravens and eagles soared in the air. Although the Navajo had come to depend on farming, they continued raiding the pueblos for material goods for more than a century. The canyon was their safe haven.

The "White House" ruins in the Canyon de Chelly in Chinle, Arizona.

The Influence of the Spanish

Before the Navajo established themselves in and around the canyon, a group of Spaniards led by Francisco Vásquez de Coronado entered their territory seeking riches, slaves, and new land. Their arrival sometime around 1541 was after fellow Spaniard Hernán Cortés had conquered Mexico. They were hungry for new success. These men called the Navajo the Querechos and respected them more than some other tribes they had encountered before.

Pedro de Castaneda accompanied Coronado, and in 1596 he wrote: "That they were very intelligent is evident from the fact that, although they conversed by means of signs they made themselves, [they] understood so well that there was no need of an interpreter."[8]

Visiting the Canyon de Chelly

Today, fewer than one hundred Navajo families actually live in the Canyon de Chelly. Part of an 83,340-acre Navajo-owned attraction, the Canyon de Chelly National Monument is managed by the National Park Service. The monument also includes Canyon del Muerto, Monument Canyon, and Black Rock Canyon, and it draws 850,000 visitors each year.

Although paved roads hug the rim of the canyon, the best way to see it is from the bottom. The canyon is dangerous for people who are not familiar with it though. There are miles of unpaved roads and quicksand along the creek bed. For that reason, non-Navajo visitors are not allowed in the canyon without a guide. Native American and other guides may be hired at the visitor's center, which is situated at the mouth of the canyon, or through nearby hotels. But no matter where they are hired, guides must be certified by the National Park Service.

At the bottom of the canyon is a winding river that supports tamarisk, Russian olive, and cottonwood trees. And within its cliffs, the ruins of the once-great Anasazi dwellings can be found. One point in the canyon that is particularly significant to the Navajo is Spider Rock. This forked spire stands alone on the canyon floor, and the tribe believes it is the home of Spider Woman, the spiritual guide who taught the Navajo to weave.

permitted them to travel faster, extended their range, and allowed their raiders to make quicker getaways. Goats provided meat, milk, and silken hairs for fine weaving, and sheep gave them meat as well as stronger wool for weaving blankets and rugs. Sheep were a most important gift, as they would come to define Navajo lives forever.

The Spaniards also brought along Catholic missionaries, who wanted to change the Navajo in another way. The Europeans, viewing the Native Americans as uncivilized, thought it was their duty to convert the "savages" to Christianity. But the missionaries did not succeed with the Navajo. Although the tribe gladly accepted the new crops the Spaniards introduced—peaches, potatoes, and wheat—they would not accept their religion. Evading missionary activities was easy for the nomadic Navajo, who routinely packed up their few belongings and moved around within the boundaries of their territory. When the priests tried to make them go to church, they simply went somewhere else.

The whole region was home to the Navajo, and the missionaries were only visitors. The Navajo had a right to live in it the way they had been taught by their holy

The Spaniards unintentionally changed Navajo ways by the modern innovations they brought with them. Metal tools and firearms would help to make planting and hunting easier for the Navajo, and horses

Spanish conquistador Francisco Vásquez de Coronado and his men wander the deserts.

people. To them, everything around them was alive, and no church could hold the spirit of Navajo religion.

Becoming One with the Land

The Dine' were a mighty people to have traveled so far and to have adapted so well. Although they came from harsh surround-ings, the new territory was harsh in a different way. Here, they had to completely change their lifestyle and learn to thrive with little water. They were smart, though. By using the techniques of the people around them, the Dine' learned not only to survive in the desert but also to prosper. Yet this sustaining lifestyle almost became part of the past.

Chapter 2

A Picture of the Dine'

Over the past few decades, the traditional Navajo lifestyle has been fading. Navajo tribespeople who attended American schools from the mid-1950s onward were influenced by modern American culture and began to feel that the "old ways" were primitive and outdated. Tribal elders and others more in tune with tradition deeply regretted the loss of the Navajo way of life and tried to reverse the trend. They urged area schools to become more involved in preserving the customs and rituals that make the Dine' unique. Today, new enthusiasm is spreading throughout the reservation. While some customs and rituals of the past are celebrated less frequently today, others have been adapted to fit a modern way of life.

One of the old ways teaches that each member of the tribe is important, so the Navajo begin learning who they are when they are very young. Even before Navajo children are born, families hold special ceremonies in their honor. On the day of their birth, the family buries the child's umbilical cord near the family home. This act symbolizes a transfer of support from their biological mother to their spiritual mother, which is Mother Earth. The family also buries the placenta, or afterbirth, near a young tree. The nutrients from the placenta nourish the tree so that it may grow with the child.

While they are working, Navajo mothers may use a cradleboard to keep their children safe and comfortable. This wooden bed has straps and padding to hold the baby in place, and it is often cut from the tree where the placenta is buried. Because the Navajo believe that there is life in all things, this practice promotes a special spiritual relationship between child and tree—a bond that should carry into adult life.

Another custom for Navajo children is to wake up very early and run east to greet the morning sun and stars. This action is said to earn the children blessings from the Holy Ones and to help them begin a fruitful day as members of the Dine' community.

A Navajo infant rests on a cradleboard. Navajo children were raised by all members of the tribe, giving children a large extended family.

In Navajo society the whole extended family is ultimately responsible for raising the children. Some may live with grandparents, aunts or uncles, or another adult blood relative with whom the children can easily communicate. In this way children reap the benefits of adult guidance beyond what they learn from their parents.

Navajo Ways of Consideration

Generosity is an important quality to all Navajo. There must always be enough food to entertain visitors, and all Navajo gatherings feature lavish meals.

The Navajo also believe in repaying generosity and good deeds. Rewarding singers who preside over spiritual and healing ceremonies is an obligation that must be met with openhandedness. Yet this is more than mere good manners; fair payment is considered necessary for a successful blessing.

Special rules are followed during Navajo religious and curing ceremonies. Even the method of entering and seating oneself while at a service is important. Participants come into the building in which a religious ceremony is held and move clockwise to match the east-to-west movement of the sun. Men sit in the south;

women sit in the north. Patients or honored guests sit in the western position, facing the door. According to a booklet published by the Southwestern Association on Indian Affairs entitled *Indians of* *the Southwest*, "The Navajo believes that his universe functions according to certain rules. If one learns these rules and lives in accordance with them, he will keep safe or be restored to safety."[9]

A White Man Who Helped the Navajo Economy

John Lorenzo Hubbell opened Hubbell's Trading Post in Ganado, Arizona, in 1876. For the first time, the Navajo had a chance to trade with the whites, and they would come from miles around to participate in the barter. But they found more than goods and a place for meeting and gossiping—they found a new way of life.

Hubbell was a smart businessman. He found that the whites liked the blankets made by the Navajo, and he saw even greater potential in the market. Hubbell prodded the Navajo women to weave on a much larger scale because he knew he could sell the big weavings for rugs at a higher price.

He recognized potential in the silver market, too. He invited Mexican silversmiths onto the reservation. They refined the knowledge Navajo men already had about working with the metal and recruited more to participate in the craft. By the 1890s turquoise became an important part of Navajo silverwork.

Hubbell's foresight continues to help Navajo craftspeople make money with their arts. Even today Hubbell's Trading Post attracts Indians and tourists alike with a variety of goods and crafts from native tribes in the area. Some things have changed, though. Instead of a booming proprietorship run by one man, Hubbell's is now a national historic site run by the National Park Service.

John Lorenzo Hubbell afforded Indians a trading post and Europeans a place to mingle, barter goods, and gossip.

One such rule is to avoid looking a person in the eye when he or she is talking. It is also considered impolite to ask people their names. Strangers may offer this information freely, or not at all, as they decide. "When a Navajo introduces himself, he tells his clan name, where he lives, his name and his occupation,"[10] says Navajo Will Tsosie Jr. But in all introductory actions, the Navajo are reserved.

Navajo people will not usually walk up and knock on someone's door. They may park their vehicle outside the dwelling and wait to be noticed. When the person inside has noted the arrival of company and has done whatever might be necessary to receive unexpected guests, he or she will politely come out to welcome the visitors.

Navajo Sociability

To the Navajo, impoliteness is intolerable. Tribespeople who act badly are said to dishonor their entire family. In 1890 a prominent Arizonan whose brother worked as an Indian agent wrote,

> To each other the Navajos are uniformly courteous, never quarreling among themselves, and conducting all their intercourse [discussion] with the utmost amity. I have never heard of one striking another in anger, and if it has ever occurred, I feel safe in saying that it has been among those who have been more or less in contact with white men.[11]

Conventions governing interaction between members of the Navajo tribe have been influenced by American culture. The Navajo have borrowed some American customs and refined them in the Navajo way.

For example, the Navajo shake hands when they wish to offer a sign of friendship. However, a Navajo handshake is more like the touching of palms, and they do not shake hands as a greeting. They usually prefer to wait for an appropriate moment, when a feeling of goodwill and friendship sparks the exchange.

Many customs practiced among the Navajo are not carried off the reservation. Navajo tribe members who live and work in other parts of the country usually follow the same social conventions as other Americans; however, some reservation practices are quite different from those followed in other parts of the United States.

Reservation Ways

Navajo people are known for puckering up and pointing with their lips. Since pointing with the index finger is held to be discourteous, it is preferable to indicate direction either with the lips or with the hand fully extended. Pointed lips can also mean that the person wants a ride, although non-Navajo visitors would miss the significance and might consider the behavior odd.

In turn, visitors' brash behavior sometimes stuns the Navajo. One practice of camera-wielding tourists is particularly offensive: "They never ask permission," said Navajo Frank Fatt. "They just stick a cam-

Pawning as a Way of Life

Reservation trading posts introduced the Navajo to "pawning." A pawn is an item such as a rug or a piece of jewelry that someone offers in exchange for money. Pawnshops and trading posts that lend people money based on the value of the pawn also store the property. To get their goods back, borrowers must repay the amount borrowed, plus interest.

When borrowers do not buy back their pawns within a set time limit, their goods become "dead pawn." Often, people leave pawns with no intention of getting them back. Regardless of the reason why pawns go dead, pawnbrokers then have the right to sell pawns, just as they would any other piece of merchandise on their shelves.

Trading posts originated the practice of pawning on the reservation when they allowed Native Americans to exchange personal and household goods for food or other necessities. Today, many Navajo use the pawning system to obtain money and other goods as well as a way to store their valuables. As long as they pay a regular fee, the pawn remains "live" but under the protection of the business owner's security and insurance.

Many Navajo still prefer pawning to banks because it is an easier, quicker way to obtain money. However, increased numbers of automated teller machines (ATMs) and bank branches on the reservation, combined with lower bank interest rates, have recently attracted more Navajo to commercial banks.

era in your face and start shooting. It's like you're not even a person."[12] When someone takes a Navajo's photo, the subject expects the photographer to ask permission first and to offer a small gratuity in return.

"Basically, Native Americans treasure their privacy just like anybody else,"[13] says George John, a police captain and member of the Navajo Nation. There are strict rules for outsiders who attend tribal social and cultural events as well. The Navajo expect guests to dress with modesty, to leave "souvenirs" like rocks and plants on the reservation, and to listen quietly.

The Navajo feel that it is especially important to pay attention to older people.

Navajo Sherry R. Curley says, "It is a basic, basic belief that the elders hold the wisdom of the tribe, and when they speak, you listen."[14] Respect for elders is fundamental to Navajo life.

In the past most Navajo rituals and customs were not written; they were kept in the hearts and minds of the people. Tribal elders had the important responsibility of teaching the Navajo way of life to the young—and there was much to learn. In the Navajo lifestyle, a precise set of rules governs all behavior, from a simple act such as waking up in the morning to a more complex activity like building a home.

Building a Hogan

The traditional Navajo home is the hogan, or hooghan, a name meaning "the place home." Although many Navajo people live in modern housing today, extended families usually have at least one hogan for religious ceremonies.

The first hogans were conical and were made from logs, tree branches, and mud. First, the builders made an excavation about the same size as the proposed structure. This hollow could be as shallow as six inches or as deep as twenty-four inches, and it allowed people to sit upright inside the hogan. Without the hollow, they would have had to lean forward along the hogan's slanted walls. The hollow also provided more room to stand and formed a shelf for storing possessions when the hogan poles were set a few inches back from its perimeter.

The next building step used forked and straight cedar logs, which were balanced top-to-top to make a tall five-sided framework. Tree branches were then piled against the supports and were coated with mud to provide insulation from cold or heat. There were no windows. These hogans with pointed frames are known as "male" hogans.

Hogan construction is symbolic. The first and most important logs in construction represent husband and wife and a

Navajo women outside their hogan, the traditional Navajo home, built with mud and tree branches.

strong marriage, and the door of the hogan always faces east to greet the morning sun. Throughout construction there are prayers and songs to make the hogan strong. Before moving in, the new owners invite family and friends for a ceremonial blessing of their home, even if they do not plan to live there permanently.

When a person dies in a hogan, the survivors abandon it and leave it to decay, along with all of the household furnishings. The Navajo believe that it would be bad luck to use these materials to rebuild or restock a new living space. Often, a hole is knocked in the north wall, and the roof is allowed to cave in. Thus, everyone will know that someone died there, and they will avoid the hogan. Even a house blessing ceremony cannot rid the hogan of such bad luck, according to the Navajo, who follow traditional ways.

Old-Style Hogans

The interior of old-style hogans had packed-earth floors and one round room. This promoted closeness of the family because everyone lived in the same space. When it was time to sleep, rolled sheepskins and blankets were unfurled on the dirt floor, which was very hard and easy to clean by sweeping.

In a one-room hogan, many family possessions were kept outside during the summer. Pots and pans usually hung outdoors,

A modern hogan, made of interlocking logs in Northwestern New Mexico.

too. During the winter it was important for all members of the family to keep their things in order since they lived together in a space smaller than one room in an average modern house.

These primitive hogans lacked electricity or indoor plumbing, so much living occurred outdoors. The sun provided daytime light, and water often had to be hauled from a river or other source, sometimes for very long distances. A hole at the top of the hogan's roof allowed smoke from the open central fire to escape.

The Hogan Today

Although some Navajo still live in this type of hogan, the home's construction changed as modern building supplies became available. Today, there are six- and eight-sided versions of the hogan. The

Some Tips on Navajo Pronunciations

Vowels:	a, e, i, o (there is no u)	Short vowels
	With accent mark (as in é)	Rise in pitch
	No mark	Neutral in tone
	Double letters (áá)	Sound should be drawn out
Consonants:	h, k, kw, l, m, n, s, t, ts, w, y, z	Pronounced as in English
	b, d, g	No breath used behind them; often heard as p, t, or k.
	j	Pronounced softly, as "zhe"
	c	Pronounced as "sh"
	dj	Pronounced as "j" in *just*
	tc	Pronounced as "ch" in *church*
	ł	Sounds like "th," but with tongue on roof of mouth, instead of the teeth

Some Navajo words and their English translations:

bilagáana	white person
dził	mountain
bááh	bread
tsé	rock
Asdzáá Nádleehé	Changing Woman
neskahi	fat
yá'át'ééh	greetings, hello

logs that form the walls are laid horizontally, end over end, and stepped in gradually toward the rounded top. The rounded top signifies a "female" hogan.

Modern hogans usually have wooden floors, although some ceremonial hogans still have floors of mud. A fifty-five gallon drum, cut in half, may support the fire, or there might be a potbellied stove. Stovepipes extend toward the top hole to carry out smoke more efficiently.

The hole is more than convenient. As with everything else about the hogan, whether old or new, it is symbolic. "That keeps us in contact with Father Sky. The dirt floor keeps us in touch with Mother Earth,"[15] says Navajo Donald Fatt.

Many people live in "female" structures and keep a "male" hogan nearby for religious ceremonies. Today, hogans and the materials used to build them vary greatly in Navajoland. A typical traditional Navajo homestead would include a hogan with a tree-shade awning. This type of awning is sometimes made from young trees and branches, and it provides shelter from the summer sun. The homestead would also include a corral for horses and sheep.

Nontraditional Housing

Although hogans are still widely used on all parts of the reservation, some Navajo people prefer to live in more modern structures, and tribe members may build any type of house they wish. Government programs established to assist Native Americans help the Navajo to buy homes.

The Department of Housing and Urban Development (HUD) erected many small tract homes on the reservation that tribespeople could buy at reasonable prices. Other programs, such as the federal Snyder Act of 1998, help needy homeowners make improvements to their homes.

The demand for modern housing is great on the reservation. Unfortunately, the funding for such housing is difficult to obtain. Overcrowding is a problem in 21 percent of reservation homes as opposed to a national average of just under 3 percent.

Because mobile homes are easier to acquire and lend themselves well to desert living, 14 percent of the Dine' live in

Children playing on a Navajo reservation near Window Rock, Arizona.

them. A familiar sight from the highway is a mobile home with old tires on the roof. Tires help to break up the desert wind as it flows over the home and stabilize it during windstorms.

Some Navajo people live in single-family dwellings, in apartments, in mobile homes, or in hogans near cities or towns while others live in desolate parts of the reservation. In these isolated spots, people still have no plumbing, electricity, or water, and they must depend on trucks to bring them water for drinking, cooking, bathing, washing clothes, and watering animals. If bad road conditions make this impossible, people must walk to a clean source and carry the water back in buckets, just as they did in the past.

No matter what type of house they live in or where on the reservation they live, the Navajo are generous with food. Even in the most modern of homes, a Navajo feast will include some traditional foods.

Navajo Favorite Foods

Mutton is a main dish in the Navajo diet, as it has been since sheep came to the Southwest. The Navajo use the meat of matured sheep to make one particular favorite: mutton stew. This dish consists of mutton chunks, potatoes, carrots, and celery in a clear broth. In addition, the Navajo use the meat of sheep and lambs to create many other dishes.

Corn is another Navajo staple. Blue corn makes pudding, tasty pancakes, and cereal, but roasted ears of white or yellow corn are also favorite foods. Another tradi-

tional recipe is dried corn soup, which is made from dried corn kernels that have been soaked in water overnight and boiled. By adding water, pork or beef, onion, red

Navajo-Churro Sheep

Churro sheep was the first breed of domesticated sheep in America. Over the years, the Spanish word *churra*, which means "scrub," became *churro*, a common mispronunciation. Today, the sheep are called Navajo-Churro to acknowledge the close connection between the breed and the people.

Navajo-Churro sheep are hearty and have unusual resistance to disease. They require no special attention and can thrive when left to their own devices on the open range. The Navajo find them invaluable because of their ability to survive on grass as well as on other desert scrub brush. One characteristic particular to this type of sheep is the tendency of rams to sport two pairs of fully developed horns. Ewes bear lambs easily, and the lambs have a high rate of survival.

The sheep also feed and warm the Navajo. When a sheep is slaughtered, every part of the animal is used. The meat has a superior flavor and a low fat content. The skin can be used for sleeping pads or covers. Even the blood, fat, and intestines are used in some recipes, and bones are given to the dogs.

chili pods, salt, and pepper, Navajo cooks make wonderfully hearty chowder.

Navajo fry bread, which dates back to the nineteenth century, came about because the whites gave Native Americans foodstuffs they had never seen before, including flour and baking powder. To create fry bread, the Navajo combine flour and baking powder with some water and a little salt and then roll the dough into a ball. Next, they flatten the ball and fry it in hot oil. The Navajo like to dip the bread into salt, and they usually serve it with mutton stew. A modern favorite is the Navajo taco, which is made by heaping green chilis, tomatoes, and cheese on top of fry bread.

Sometimes modern Navajo people eat like all other Americans. In fact, one of the loveliest vistas in Navajoland is from the Navajo-staffed McDonald's restaurant outside of Page, Arizona. The Navajo like fast food, too.

A Glimpse of Navajo Fashion

Modern Navajo tribespeople also dress like other Americans. They wear blue jeans and athletic shoes, business suits, or any other ready-to-wear garments offered at retail stores across the nation. Derived from clothing given to the Navajo by the federal government in the late nineteenth century, time-honored Navajo dress for men consists of loose trousers and calico or velveteen shirts. Women wear long tiered or full skirts, velveteen blouses, and high-topped moccasins. Today, many still wear these outfits to traditional ceremonies; for everyday wear, they may combine elements of this traditional style with modern clothing.

But whether they are male or female, the Navajo love to accent their traditional clothing with lots of jewelry. Silver concho belts, rings and bracelets with huge chunks of turquoise, and necklaces made from strands of turquoise and coral are all popular. Rather than being mere accessories, these pieces are symbols. In the past the amount of jewelry people wore indicated their financial status; expensive, well-crafted pieces were the work of master Navajo silversmiths.

The Beginning of a New Way of Life

The Dine' discovered that they were fine craftspeople when whites began to buy their work a century ago. Around that time they made all types of jewelry, using American and Spanish coins and raw silver. When they added the bluish green mineral known as turquoise to the silver, the jewelry's appeal increased and became much more popular both within and outside of the tribe.

Rug weaving is another admired craft of the Dine'. Navajo rugs are highly prized for their pleasing and often colorful designs as well as their durability. Different rug patterns come from different regions. The Ganado pattern from eastern Arizona has bright red and black geometric designs with touches of white and gray. Two Grey Hills rugs include more intricate designs and are crafted in lighter earthy tones.

A Navajo rug weaver on a New Mexico reservation. The Navajo have bartered and sold these ornate rugs for hundreds of years.

All-American Indians

Aside from traditional ways of earning income, about 30 percent of the Navajo population has left the reservation to earn a living. Not many depend on farming to sustain their families anymore, and craftwork income is sporadic and sometimes meager. Modern Navajo people may be lawyers, doctors, police officers, food servers, administrative assistants, or fill any occupation that any other American might follow today, including service in national or local government.

The wool used in making these rugs, as well as the mutton and lamb that the Navajo eat, comes from a breed known as Navajo-Churro sheep. They are descended from the Spanish Churra sheep and have a long outer coat and a soft undercoat. This affords the sheep ideal protection from the harsh desert climate, which can be freezing in winter and sizzling in summer. Their wool is special because it contains little lanolin, or natural oil. Therefore, rug makers can process the wool without having to clean the oil from it first, which saves time and energy. When woven, the wool has a fine luster.

Although the Dine' constantly renew their world, they are able to stay the same, just as their mythical parent Changing Woman renews herself with each new season. They may look like other Americans in the way they dress, or they may combine old styles with new. They often choose to eat the foods other Americans eat. They follow various occupations, just like other Americans. And they have the same rights and privileges. Yet the Navajo have their own special identity. Their traditional culture defines them, and their religion is more than a system of beliefs—it is a way of life.

Chapter 3

Navajo Spirituality

The word *religion* does not exist in the Navajo language. Rather than a separation of daily life and spiritual life, traditional Navajo live their religion every day. Their goal is to be in balance with the universe. Terms like *good* and *evil* do not exist for them; there is only *harmony* or *disharmony*. The Navajo believe a person's actions influence the balance of the universe; so, to assure that harmony and joy continue, they strive to "walk in beauty."

Hozho is a Navajo term that describes humankind's balance with the universe and all its beauty. The Navajo believe that all things in nature are interrelated and interact according to this order. Therefore, it is important for them to maintain *hozho* to keep not only their own lives but also the animals, plants, and environment around them safe and peaceful. Plants, trees, and flowers are seen as the earth's clothing. Even bugs and animals are important; each has its place in the scheme of things. Traditionalists see the whole world and all of nature as alive and sacred.

Keeping balance involves many rituals and songs, which traditional Navajo perform as they follow their day-to-day lives. Corn and corn pollen are also part of Navajo religion and everyday life. Many people still walk out of their home each morning and throw a bit of cornmeal into the sky. "It's an offering to our gods for protection,"[16] says Navajo Roger Begay. This action is also a petition to the spirits for guidance during the day, and it is believed to promote prosperity and fertility.

The land is very important to the Navajo, too. Their whole spiritual being is tied to the land, and many landmarks are sacred. From the mountains that limit them, called "Those-Who-Stand-Under-the-Sky," to the place where the "First People" emerged, called the "Center-of-the-Earth," all of Navajoland is holy. Navajo Norman Tulley explains: "The Earth, you were born from it, it gave you the sacred flesh. That's how the Earth is: it feeds you, it gives you animals, it gives you plants, it gives you shelter."[17]

The balance of nature may be disrupted by something simple: Perhaps one person is rude to another. Even the acts of offenders who do not realize they have been rude can create an imbalance. Contrary to European thought, Navajo people can even be held responsible for their dreams. A bad dream involving death, a snakebite, lightning, or even a mishap in making a piece of silver jewelry could mean sickness, accidental injury, or worse to the party involved. To eliminate the effects of these actions, a "sing" or "chant" is usually called for so that the people involved can once again "walk in beauty." In the Navajo lifestyle, such rituals are like herbs and oils: forms of medicine that cure spiritual as well as physical ills.

Traditional Medicine Ways

Before preparations for a sing or chant begin, and if the illness is not too severe, patients or their families might consult herbalists. These people will work with patients, who may need to take herbal cures internally, by mouth or inhalation, or as salves and ointments on their skins. If the symptoms do not subside, patients may then call in another person to diag-

The Mystical, Magical Number Four

As with other Native American tribes, the number four is significant to the Navajo. It has significance in their creation story and in everyday life: There are four worlds, four basic colors, four sacred stones, and four sacred mountains. These are some other examples of how the number four fits into the lives of the Navajo:

- There are four primary directions: east, south, west, north.
- Four winds blow: white or east, blue or south, yellow or west, black or north.
- Four seasons exist in nature: spring, summer, autumn, winter.
- Changing Woman created four original clans: the Near Water People, the Mud People, the Bitter Water People, the Salt Water People.
- There are four sacred rivers: the Rio Grande, the Colorado, the Little Colorado, the San Juan.

The number four also dictates certain customs:

- The Navajo may ask for something only four times.
- After a ceremony, there is usually a four-day quarantine period before the one "sung over" can return to daily life.
- A Navajo may not tell the truth when questioned three times, but must be honest the fourth time.
- Burials must take place within four days of death.

nose the problem. The Navajo call these people "diviners," "crystal gazers," "star gazers," or "hand tremblers."

In *Navajo Religion: A Study of Symbolism,* natural scientist Gladys A. Reichard describes how the trembler works: "The diviner [seer] is seized with shaking, beginning usually with gentle tremors of arms or legs and gradually spreading until the whole body shakes violently."[18] While in a trembling state, the seer enters a trancelike state, concentrating on the cause of the patient's illness.

When a diviner determines what is wrong with the patient, he or she will prescribe certain ceremonies for certain conditions. For instance, if the trouble originated because someone hurt a snake (even unintentionally), a "Holyway" chant might be in order. Snakes are considered a destructive force, and illness or imbalance can result from injuries done to them. A "Lifeway" chant is prescribed for injuries received in an accident, and people having trouble with bears will ask for a "Mountainway" chant.

Once the cause of a problem has been determined, the family will then hire a singer, or *hataalii,* who has been trained in healing methods passed down over centuries in the Navajo culture. "[The *hataalii*] is a center that receives power from all proper sources and distributes it to all worthy subscribers [believers],"[19] says Reichard. Whereas the diviner is believed to possess supernatural gifts, the *hataalii*'s influence stems from knowledge.

The Hataalii: His Power, His Equipment

The *hataalii*'s power helps to heal the body by healing the spirit as well.

Reichard says that cures are primarily for the spirit, but "the Navajo calls upon his gods to restore not only his head, his breast, his fingertips, his limbs, and his body, but also the tip of his tongue, his voice and sound, his breath, his power of motion, and his mind."[20] To the Navajo, no part of any individual is less important than any other. If the body of the patient is healed but not the spirit, there has been no proper cure. To complete the treatment the *hataalii* sometimes requires the patient to sit or sleep inside a sandpainting, an intricate design created in sand that is believed to hold special curative powers.

The *hataalii* usually learns his job by apprenticing with an established *hataalii,* and the lessons continue for many years. He learns rituals and methods of sandpainting, which are vital to the success of any ceremony. He is also taught about sacred plants and the proper manner in which to collect them. He also learns many songs.

Unlike European religious ceremonies, which usually are completed in a matter of hours, Navajo sings may last from three to nine days. There are so many different rituals involved in each chant that most *hataalii* are usually proficient in only a few, and people must hire different singers for different cures.

For each ceremony, the *hataalii* must gather fresh plants and herbs. In addition, he comes to a sing with a chanter's bundle, which includes all of the equipment needed to perform the ceremony. Each bundle is specific to the sing to be performed and is

Because the Navajo believe that earth has "drawing power"—that is, that it is capable of draining energy—chant items cannot touch the ground. Several baskets hold these items until they are needed, keeping their sacred power intact. These containers are often made from precious stone like whiteshell or turquoise and have rims in a contrasting colored stone like jet or redstone. People holding the ceremony may purchase baskets, use family heirlooms, or make the baskets themselves for the occasion. So many baskets are needed, however, that the person holding the sing often must borrow baskets from friends or relatives.

Some Frequently Held Ceremonies

A Navajo medicine man works on a sandpainting, part of the curing ceremony for an ailing member of the tribe.

prepared differently. Some of the items in the bundle will be prayer sticks. These are short strips of carefully selected wood, which may be decorated with paint, beads, feathers, precious stones, or tobacco. Another item is a bull roarer, an elliptically shaped and decorated wooden block. When tied to a string and whirled around in the air, it makes a noise like the powerful cry of a bull. Some bundles may contain arrows, bows, and rattles.

The "Blessingway" is a ceremony that covers many occasions, including the coming birth of a child or the departure of a man going off to a war. Sometimes a Blessingway is held for its own sake, without a specific focal event. Central to this ceremony is the Navajo creation story. It puts those who attend in tune with the Holy Ones and promotes good luck and prosperity. Many of the songs used in other chants originated in the Blessingway, and its effects are so strong that at least one song in every ceremony will be a Blessingway song.

Another ritual is the "Enemyway," which was originally held for men returning from battle but is also used to counteract the bad effects of violence. The Enemyway is also said to be effective when a Navajo contracts illness from a non-Navajo person. Surprisingly, a highlight of this ceremony is a dance involving young women of marriageable age. This tradition stems from the cultural belief that it was good to introduce young marriageable women to warriors returning from battle. In the past, and sometimes even today on the reservation, this dance is called the Squaw Dance. Since *squaw* is considered a derogatory term by most Native American women, Girl Dance is now the festivity's preferred name.

During the Girl Dance, a young woman selects the partner of her choice. The man cannot refuse to dance with her, otherwise the girl's female relatives may verbally abuse him. If the man is not interested in the woman who chose him, he may only stop dancing after offering her a small present or some money. If the woman finds she is unhappy with her choice, she must steal one of the man's personal possessions and sell it back to him. When she receives the token payment, the couple may part. Before a young woman can participate in this gala, however, she must be honored as an adult.

The Art of Sandpainting

Navajo sandpainting, also called drypainting, consists of creating intricate designs in colored sand or in powdered vegetable or mineral material. More than five hundred traditional sandpainting patterns exist; however, there are no illustrations of them on paper. To practice the profession, a singer must memorize the method of making the many paintings. He is privately trained in the proper techniques by an experienced *hataalii*. When instructional sandpaintings are made, a detail is intentionally changed or left out. This prevents the image from becoming sacred.

There are several different sandpaintings for each chant. Yet singers do not use every image each time they perform a ceremony. Singers choose sandpaintings to suit each patient. Once the chant has ended, singers destroy their sandpaintings in the same order they were created. The used sand is then collected and released into the wind.

Navajo sandpainting has also become a popular form of Southwestern art. Commercial sandpaintings are made by applying layers of sand to wood that has been coated with glue. Some sandpaintings include scenes from real life; others resemble sacred images used in Navajo chantways with color changes or misplaced figures. They are sold in trading posts, specialty stores, and art galleries around the world.

The Kinaalda is held to mark a woman's coming to maturity, and it honors and repeats the observance held for Changing Woman of Navajo mythology. A woman becomes eligible to receive this blessing after reaching puberty and before she is married. It lasts four days. During this time, older women teach the young woman what is expected of her as an adult. Traditionally, these lessons included instruction on becoming a good wife and mother and lessons in weaving. Today, the ceremony focuses more on what the young woman needs to become a responsible adult, no matter what life path she chooses. All of this helps her to "walk in beauty" as an adult.

Other Ceremonial Considerations

Some Navajo ceremonies are intimate, involving only patients and their immediate families; others offer a good reason for people to get together. These rites may draw a large crowd, including visitors who are not members of the tribe. Since feeding all of the guests is an important tradition and few Navajo today are wealthy, current etiquette dictates that each guest bring a gift of food, such as a can of coffee or some soft drinks. Visitors may bring cash instead of food.

The cost of nourishment for the guests, plus a sizable fee for the *hataalii*, may run

Navajo dancers at the Intertribal Indian Ceremonial in Gallup, New Mexico.

Navajo Words: What They Mean and How to Say Them

WORD	MEANING	PRONUNCIATION
Dine'	the People	di-NEH
Dinetah	Navajoland	di-neh-TAH
Diyin Dine'	Holy People	DEE-un di-NEH
	(the Navajo divinities)	
haigo	winter	HAY-go
hogan	house	HO-gahn
łizhin	black	she-ZHIN
naadą́ą́	corn	na-a-DAA
séí	sand	SAYEE
sin	songs	sin
sodizin	prayers	so-da-ZIN

into the thousands of dollars for a nine-day event. However, it is not customary for the singer to set his own fee. He receives payment based on the family's financial standing and usually accepts what is offered after some discussion. The payment may include gifts of livestock or material goods instead of or in addition to cash, and the proper amount is considered important for the blessing to have the right effect.

According to the booklet *Indians of the Southwest,*

> Should a given ceremonial fail to cure the sickness, it merely indicates that the offense has not been properly traced, and the source must be further sought. There may be numerous chants performed until the patient recovers, or dies. Death is considered to be beyond human calculation [control]. When death of a patient becomes certain, the officiating singer withdraws before the inevitable.[21]

The Navajo do not fear death any more than people of any other culture. Yet they fear the dead because of the traditional belief that dead people can become ghosts and transfer the "ghost sickness," or *chindi* (which means "bad luck" or "the devil"). Traditional custom sets a period of four days during which it is forbidden to speak the name of a person who has just died. To mention the name of someone so recently deceased might attract the attention of the person's ghost, which is unthinkable. If traditional Navajo see or even dream of a ghost, they require a proper ceremony to assure their own continued existence.

Not all modern Navajo people hold these traditional beliefs about healing and death. Many prefer modern solutions for medical problems. The federal government offers health care assistance to all Native Americans who request it.

Attitudes About Modern Medicine

Many Navajo have come to trust twentieth-century medicine. In fact, they have their own health service, which is administered by the Indian Health Service (IHS), an agency of the U.S. Department of Health and Human Services. "The Navajo Area IHS Office, located in Window Rock, Arizona, administers numerous clinics, health centers, and hospitals, providing health care to 201,583 members of the Navajo Nation."[22] Navajo families and their dependents can receive routine care at any of these facilities, free of charge.

Ceremony is important in Navajo tradition. Here, a girl in full regalia dances at the Red Earth Festival in Oklahoma City.

Traditionally oriented Navajo shun hospitals, calling them "houses of the dead." This phrase reflects the observation that many people die in hospitals, but it fails to acknowledge that patients who were gravely ill would have died soon, if not sooner, in any location. Some younger people are torn between two worlds. Although they visit doctors when ill, they may have a chant performed to accompany modern medical care. It is difficult for people raised in the traditional Navajo culture to completely trust modern doctors. Nonetheless, one young medical intern described his experience with the Navajo this way: "The patients . . . were by and large wonderful, grateful folks whose untiring, but largely unsuccessful, efforts to teach me Navajo touched my heart."[23]

Non-Navajo Religions on the Reservation

Although not all Navajo practice the traditional religion, most still uphold some part of the culture. As with medicine, many Navajo still combine the best of both worlds. One young boy explained it this way: "You know more about life from different points of view. When you have a hard decision to make, it's easier to determine what's right because it's usually the choice taught by both cultures."[24]

The largest non-Navajo religion on the reservation is Mormonism, which stands to reason since the Mormon Church is based in Utah and the Mormons have been aggressive missionaries for more than one hundred years. Catholic and Protestant Navajo also exist as well as those who follow the Native American Church. This church has been the source of controversy for many years because its religious ceremonies include the use of a controlled substance called peyote. When the tribal government outlawed the use of this drug in 1940, many members of the church were arrested; however, in 1994 the U.S. government restored the Native American Church's right to use the drug, citing the right to religious freedom.

This was one instance in which the federal government was helpful to Native Americans. But for much of the nineteenth century, the U.S. government and many Native American tribes were at war. This war included the Dine', and it drastically changed their way of life.

Chapter 4

The Long Walk and Back

The Navajo had always believed that the land among the four sacred mountains was where they would live forever. From the early 1600s to the mid-1800s life followed a familiar pattern. Some members of the tribe busily cultivated their fields, tended their sheep, and followed their life of *hozho* without much regard for the world around them. These were the *ricos*—people whose wealth could be measured in horses, sheep, and goats. Others, who interacted with the neighbors, were called *ladrones,* which is a Spanish word meaning "thieves." For hundreds of years the Navajo had raided settlements in Mexican territory in addition to stealing from the pueblos.

The Mexican army had long tried to control the *ladrones.* In 1846, however, Mexico became involved in a war with the United States because the two countries could not agree on a border. While the army was busy fighting in the war, the Navajo had more freedom to raid, and their raiding activity increased.

By the terms of the Treaty of Guadalupe Hidalgo, which ended the Mexican–American War in 1848, the United States was ceded a portion of Mexican territory. After the war settlers in that territory, who had since become American citizens, appealed to the U.S. government to restrain the Navajo from making their frequent raids. Government officials did not know that the raiding had been two-sided, however. The griping settlers had also been abducting Navajo tribespeople and forcing them into slavery. The Navajo were at a disadvantage in the situation. They were not citizens because at that time it was not possible for a Native American to be a citizen of the United States.

The treaty with Mexico opened the door for American citizens such as miners and other settlers to move into and through the Navajo lands. To protect these and all other American citizens from Navajo raiding, U.S. officials first decided to try for peace and used standard American methods of making treaties to indicate a desire for friendship and understanding.

Throwaway Treaties

The U.S. government made several treaties with men whom they perceived to be Navajo tribal leaders. Still, the raiding continued, and government officials took these treaty violations as indications of bad faith on the part of the Navajo tribe. This interpretation, however, was incorrect. What the Americans could not understand was that the Navajo Nation had no single leader who was empowered to bind everyone to observe the terms of a treaty. There were leaders of small groups all over the territory. When one leader signed a treaty, other bands of Navajo had no part in that particular agreement.

But the U.S. government was determined to make these treaties stick. In 1849, for example, U.S. senator James Calhoun, accompanied by army colonel John Washington and a group of soldiers, came to Navajo country to find the principal leaders they thought existed in the Navajo Nation. They set up camp south of Two Grey Hills and cut down the Navajo's ripe corn to feed their livestock, advising the farmers that this action constituted reimbursement for their trip. As a result, the Navajo stood by and did not prevent the army from appropriating their winter food supply.

The next day five Navajo leaders came into the U.S. Army camp for a conference.

War between Mexico and the United States, incited by the battle at the Alamo and other territorial disputes, left the Navajo free to raid their neighbors.

Among them was the revered Navajo chief Narbona. According to Lieutenant James H. Simpson, who was present at the meeting, Narbona was more than eighty years old at the time and had "a grave and contemplative countenance not unlike, as many of the officers remarked (I hope the comparison will be pardoned), that of General [George] Washington."[25]

Narbona had watched some of the fighting between the United States and Mexico during the war. The force of the U.S. Army impressed him so greatly that he

Navajo chief Narbona, who was killed after a dispute over the theft of a horse.

spread the word to settle for peace, thinking the Navajo were no match for the army's military might.

By his counsel, Navajo leaders agreed to permit U.S. citizens to travel freely through their territory and to allow the government to build forts on their land without reprisal. In return, the government agreed to supply the Navajo with "presents" from time to time, such as farming equipment and blankets. When they had settled these matters, the meeting was concluded.

Tempers Rise, Many Are Killed

As the Navajo left, a volunteer soldier from New Mexico complained that a Navajo had stolen his horse. Without determining the validity of this claim, Colonel Washington insisted that the mount be surrendered to the New Mexican. The Navajo tried to defuse the situation by saying that the man with the horse in question had already left. Upon hearing that, Washington ordered that his men seize a horse from the Navajo as compensation. As the soldiers approached the group, the Navajo, assuming that they were under attack, began to gallop away. The colonel then ordered his troops to open fire, and Narbona and six other men were killed.

The killings understandably upset Narbona's son-in-law, Manuelito.

Manuelito: Last of the Resistance

Although Kit Carson and his troops captured and killed many Navajo, groups of resisters hid where soldiers could not find them. Some of their leaders were Barboncito, Ganado Mucho, and the last to surrender, Manuelito.

In April 1864 Manuelito tried to make a compromise, and he sent a messenger to Fort Canby. Manuelito said that he would settle his people near the fort, but only if the army would allow them to farm and raise sheep. In *Bury My Heart at Wounded Knee*, author Dee Brown quotes General Carleton's brusque refusal: "There is but one place for you, and that is to go to the Bosque Redondo."

Manuelito refused, worried that the army took Navajo people there to be shot. He then asked to speak with an old friend, Herrero Grande, who had already been sent to the camp. When Carleton heard that Manuelito might surrender, he sent Grande and three other men to meet with him. Grande pleaded with Manuelito, saying that if he did not surrender, the soldiers would kill them. Manuelito insisted that his god and his mother lived in the West, and he would not leave. He sent his cold and starving people back into hiding.

Upon hearing this news, Carleton became more adamant about catching Manuelito and his band. Although other Navajo were still resisting, Carleton's false impression was that Manuelito was the leader of the entire Navajo Nation. He thought that Manuelito's capture would mean that the other resisters would follow. So, he said that if Manuelito could not be captured, he was to be shot down. Finally, emaciated and nearly naked, with one arm hanging limp at his side from a terrible wound, Manuelito surrendered with twenty-three others just sixty-six days before Carleton was removed from his post.

To add to his discontent, the United States built Fort Defiance near the present-day eastern Arizona–New Mexico border. The Navajo and the army were constantly competing for pastureland for their livestock. Manuelito begged the army to leave the sparse grazing land for the Navajo, saying that the army had wagons and horses to carry feed while the Navajo would have to walk to find suitable grazing land for their many sheep and other animals. Despite his pleas, the soldiers did not stop their livestock from grazing in the nearest convenient pastures.

Manuelito and other headmen, including Ganado Mucho and Barboncito, had had enough. Manuelito proclaimed, "I will lead the Dine'. We will make war, and drive the white men from our land!"[26] He and a group of more than one thousand men laid seige to Fort Defiance in April 1860. Although they made a valiant effort and came close to winning the battle, their attack failed.

Manuelito, last of the great Navajo chiefs, led the final rebellion against the invading European settlers.

all directions and were shot and bayoneted."[27] The Navajo observed the traditional four-day period during which the names of the dead could not be mentioned and then turned to consider their uncertain future. Despite the bad omen of the deaths of women and children at Fort Fauntleroy, the Navajo did not know that the worst upheaval in their history was about to begin. Its path had been set thirty years before.

Carleton and the Indian Removal Act

In 1831 a federal law called the Indian Removal Act had authorized the president to force Native Americans to move from their homelands and resettle on reservations. The intention of moving the Native Americans to other parts of the country was twofold. First, the government sought to assimilate Native Americans by teaching them the ways of American culture and Christianity. Native Americans were then restricted to reservations, which made controlling them easier. Second, and most importantly, the government wanted Native American land, which was either more desirable for settling or was loaded with natural resources.

To make matters worse, a horse race at Fort Fauntleroy (later called Fort Wingate) in 1861 ended in violence. The Navajo accused the soldiers involved in the race of cheating, a great disturbance arose, and the fort's commander ordered his men to open fire on the Navajo. Twelve Navajo women and children were killed. Captain Nicholas Hodt wrote about what he saw: "The Navajos, squaws, and children ran in

Colonel James H. Carleton, who came into New Mexico as U.S. military leader in 1862, was empowered by the Indian Removal Act to "remove" the Navajo people. Carleton had heard stories about the southwestern gold that was waiting to be claimed by the new landowners, and he was anxious to obtain it for the United States. In June 1863 he wrote a letter to Captain Joseph Walker at the Walker Mines in Arizona: "The surveyor general of New Mexico proceeds to visit your new gold regions, and when he returns will make an official report on their probable extent and value, so that the government can be well informed on the subject." To secure the land, he planned to rid the territory of all Native Americans. In the same letter, he states, "I am just commencing active operations against the Navajoes [sic]."[28]

With full legal powers to fulfill his design, Carleton enlisted the help of famed westerner Christopher "Kit" Carson, who was then a colonel in the New Mexico cavalry. In describing his qualifications for the assignment, Carson writes: "I came to this country in 1826, and since that time have become pretty well acquainted with the Indian tribes, both in peace and at war."[29]

In June Carleton sent Carson into the field with an ultimatum for the Navajo:

Tell them they can have until the twentieth day of July of this year to come in [to surrender to army control]. . . . But after that day every Navajo that is seen will be considered as hostile and treated accordingly; that after that day the door now open will be closed. Tell them to say all this to their people, and that as sure as that the sun shines all this will come true.[30]

Navajo men, women, and children were to be brought first to Fort Wingate and then to a place called Bosque Redondo, or "Round Woody." Here, Carleton intended to "civilize" them in captivity. Any Navajo who did not comply would suffer.

Christopher "Kit" Carson sent the remaining Navajo rebels an ultimatum: surrender or be hunted down.

Carson's Path of Destruction

Kit Carson was unable to deliver Carleton's ultimatum to all of the members of the Navajo tribe, however, because they were so scattered throughout the rugged territory. He writes, "There are canyons in their country thirty miles in length, with walls a thousand feet high."[31] Many of the Navajo did not know anything about Carleton's order, let alone that they had a deadline. When the old chiefs finally learned that the army was after them, they were not so easily frightened. They told their people, "If the Americans come to take us, we will kill them."[32]

Carson first tried to starve the Navajo people into submission. He and some Mexican and Ute mercenaries, who were historically enemies of the Navajo, went about killing livestock and burning fields and orchards. They poisoned wells and destroyed hogans. They left the Navajo with few resources to survive the approaching winter of 1863–1864, which would prove to be a severe season.

Many Navajo died that year. Desperate tribespeople hid on mesas and in Canyon de Chelly, where they froze to death, starved, or died from illness. In January 1864 Carson sent a troop of men into one end of the canyon while he and his troop entered from the other. In his book *Bury My Heart at Wounded Knee,* author Dee Brown states, "From rims and ledges hun-

Carson's Mixed Emotions

Kit Carson had been in the West for nearly forty years when General Carleton ordered him to war against the Navajo Nation. Carson had been a trapper, a guide, and had spent a great deal of time among Native Americans. His first two wives were Arapaho and Cheyenne, and he had great sympathy for Native American troubles.

In fact, Carson blamed much of the difficulty with Native Americans on whites. In an 1865 report to the U.S. Congress, he wrote, "For instance, at times large trains come out to this country, and some man without any responsibility is hired to guard the horses, mules, and stock of the trains; these cattle by his negligence frequently stray off; always, if anything is lost, the cry is raised that the Indians stole it." He also knew that there was an ongoing war between the Mexicans and the Navajo.

Rather than follow Carleton's orders to pursue and kill or capture Navajo people, Carson tried to resign, complaining that he had volunteered to fight in the Civil War, not to fight against Native Americans. Yet fame was important to Carson, an uneducated man from a small town who craved the limelight. To the bedevilment of the Navajo, this overwhelming desire for respect and recognition pulled Carson back. He withdrew his resignation and followed Carleton's orders.

dreds of half-starved Navajos hurled stones, pieces of wood, and Spanish curses upon the heads of the soldiers. But they could not stop them."[33] Many Navajo were mercilessly killed; the rest were taken prisoner. An orchard of more than five thousand peach trees was burned, and all animals found wandering on the floor of the canyon were confiscated or destroyed.

IN COMMEMORATION OF THE NAVAJOS WHO LIVED HERE IN EXILE, 1863-1868.
THE CENTENNIAL RE-ENACTMENT OF THE SIGNING OF THE TREATY OF PEACE (1 JUNE 1868) TOOK PLACE ON THIS SPOT.
ERECTED BY THE NAVAJO TRIBE AND THE PLATEAU SCIENCES SOCIETY, WINDOW ROCK, ARIZONA, FEBRUARY 1971.

Memorial to the thousands of Navajo who lived in exile at Bosque Redondo.

Horrors of the Long Walk and Bosque Redondo

By early March around 3,000 Navajo had surrendered to either Fort Wingate or Fort Canby (the new name of Fort Defiance). Also that month, the Navajo began a forced march to Bosque Redondo, some 250 miles away. According to army records, 1,430 Navajo set out on the first wave, but only 1,417 arrived at their destination. During the trek, three children were kidnapped; the rest died. Some of them were murdered. According to one Dine' elder, "Women and children traveled on foot. That's why we call it the Long Walk. It was inhuman because the Navajos, if they got tired and couldn't continue to walk further, were just shot down."[34] Even women who gave birth along the way could not rest, and if they could not continue, they were killed.

During the three phases of the Long Walk, hundreds of Navajo died or disappeared. The second phase comprised 2,400 Navajo. Of them, 197 died before reaching Bosque Redondo. During the third wave of the march, a vicious storm arose that lasted four days. Nearly naked, 110 Navajo died from exposure to the cold.

Carleton was not dismayed, however, writing at the time, "Once the tribe is quietly settled on the fine reservation alluded to [Bosque Redondo], there is no reason why they will not be the most happy and prosperous and well-provided for Indians in the United States."[35]

The Navajo who made it to Bosque Redondo found little peace and joy; their traditional enemies, the Mescalero Apache, had already been brought to the camp, and the Comanche raided it often. Basic living conditions were appalling: Drinking water was full of alkali and caused great intestinal distress. In addition, although the land was barren and not suitable for farming, officials expected the Native Americans to grow crops for food. Indeed, the commander at the camp suggested that the Native Americans not be fed in order to encourage them to work to feed themselves. When meat and grain were provided, the food was low quality. Firewood was also practically nonexistent, forcing the Native Americans to dig up and burn mesquite roots.

A major problem at Bosque Redondo concerned shelter. Carleton had adobe buildings erected for the prisoners to live in, but once a Navajo died inside one of them, the structures became uninhabitable for other tribe members. Since there was no material available for hogan construction, Navajo tribe members whose traditional beliefs forced them to abandon a hut in which one of their number had died became homeless. They dug holes in the ground and covered themselves with thorny brush and dirt for what little protection these materials could provide.

By September 1864 the Navajo were forced to exist on one-half pound of meat and one-half pound of corn or bread per day. Their entire crop of three thousand acres of corn had failed as a result of infestation with armyworms, and there were not enough other foods to keep the people from starving. General Carleton wrote letters to the adjutant general of the U.S. Army and to the commissioner of the Bureau of Indian Affairs, asking for food and clothing for the Native Americans at the camp, saying they would surely die if his requests were not met. Still, there was never enough. Items that were supposed to have been delivered to the camp never appeared.

A Government-Imposed Solution

The Navajo spent four long years at the camp before reports of the deplorable conditions became widely known in Washington. As a result, Carleton was relieved of his command. By that time, one-fourth of the Dine' people had died. In 1868, after two years of investigation into the nightmare at Bosque Redondo, a delegation headed by famed Civil War general William T. Sherman went to meet with Dine' leaders. Barboncito, one of the Navajo leaders, told Sherman, "If we are taken back to our own country, we will call you our father and mother. If you should only tie a goat there, we would all live off it, all of the same opinion. I am speaking for the whole tribe, for their animals, from the horse to the dog, also the unborn."[36]

After much discussion, the treaty signed at Bosque Redondo in 1868 established a reservation for the Navajo in the midst of their traditional homeland, situated at the northern boundaries of Arizona and New Mexico. However, there were conditions to the agreement that were not favorable to the Navajo people. Their territory would be reduced by three-fourths, down to 3.5 million acres for a population of about thirty thousand, and they would not be permitted to settle permanently anywhere else. This reservation would be presided over by a government agency that would enforce the law, and forts, roads, or railroads could be built on the land. The Navajo could never again conduct raids. Moreover, they would have to agree to send all of their children who were between the ages of six and sixteen to white schools.

The Dine' accepted these terms and were to be provisioned with seeds, livestock, and farming equipment to help them start over. They returned to the land they loved, and when they neared home, Manuelito said, "When we saw the top of the mountain from Albuquerque, we wondered if it was our mountain, and we felt like talking to the ground, we loved it so, and some of the old men and women cried with joy when they reached their homes."[37]

Adjustments to the Treaty

It was not long, however, before the seemingly huge expanse of the reservation created by the treaty at Bosque Redondo seemed too small. As the Navajo population grew, their herds grew, and the animals needed more grazing land than the treaty had made available. Some Navajo people simply moved beyond the boundaries of their allotted territory to accommodate their stock.

Government agents determined that forcing these people back onto the reservation would be dangerous. The livestock would have nothing to eat, meaning the food and fiber resource the Navajo counted on to survive would be lost. Returning the Navajo to the reservation, which now seemed tiny in proportion to their need for land, could mean terrible poverty or even death from starvation.

Instead, the government decided to let these Navajo remain in place. In 1878 it enlarged the reservation by 960,000 acres to include the new homesteads. However, it was not a final solution; the tribe kept growing.

Thus, the U.S. government's attempt to craft a lasting settlement with the Navajo was only partially successful. The Navajo regained ties to the land, and to this day the treaty signed at Bosque Redondo has not been broken, but the price has been high: no longer autonomous, the Navajo became dependents of the federal government.

Chapter 5

The Navajo and the U.S. Government

When the Dine' returned home after their confinement at Bosque Redondo, things seemed the same, but they were much different. The Navajo, like other tribes before them, had been "adopted" by the United States. In many instances, the federal government would be deciding what was best for the Navajo people.

Thirty-seven years prior to the treaty at Bosque Redondo, Supreme Court justice John Marshall had described the government's attitude toward Native Americans. He wrote that they were not foreign nations within the boundaries of the United States; they were "domestic" dependent nations. "They are in a state of pupilage [like students]; their relation to the United States resembles that of a ward to his guardian."[38]

This line of thinking led to certain "paternal" or protective provisions in the U.S. treaty with the Navajo tribe. One of these made the U.S. government responsible for furnishing material goods such as farm implements and certain articles of clothing that the Dine' could not manufacture themselves. In another stipulation, the government agreed to an annual allotment of funds for each Navajo person engaged in farming or practical activities such as rug making. This money was to be held in trust by the commissioner of the Bureau of Indian Affairs (BIA), who would purchase items for the Navajo people as he saw fit.

This relationship of guardian and ward continues to exist between the BIA and the Navajo tribe to this day. The BIA maintains roads, a police force, and schools, and it holds $23 million in a Navajo Nation trust account.

The Navajo Reject Government Policies

Now seventh-generation government wards, the Navajo have made great strides in establishing their own political structure. Still, they are reluctant to pull away from government programs completely. This reluctance does not stem from an expectation or desire to be "taken care of." The Dine' simply know that they are not ready for such a step, and they want to avoid mistakes made by other tribes in the past. The Dine' have been, and continue to be, understandably cautious.

Termination is a word used to describe the process of making Native Americans self-dependent, and it means the eventual end to all federal programs on the reservations. The first step toward termination was taken in 1887, when Congress passed the Dawes General Allotment Act. According to the act, a set share of tribal land was to be granted to any Native American adult who desired it. The Native American claimants would own the land, and as property owners, they would also become American citizens. Of course, that meant that they would have to abide by federal, state, and local laws, and they would have to pay the appropriate taxes. Many Native Americans accepted the deal. They wanted to be self-sufficient, and they hoped to get away from government control. The Navajo, however, were wary of any new plans the government made for them, and they chose not to divide their reservation among the Dine'.

In 1934 another law addressed some problems introduced by the Dawes act. The Wheeler-Howard Act, also known as the Indian Reorganization Act, was developed "to promote tribal self-government by encouraging tribes to adopt constitutions and to form federally chartered corporations."[39] It also stopped the sale of the unclaimed Native American land, returned

it to the tribes, and established a system of federal loans to help tribes succeed economically. Still distrustful of the government and its officials, the Dine' voted to reject the corporation idea; to this day, the tribe has no constitution.

More than sixty years later, the Navajo are still not anxious to pursue termination, even though it would mean the end of governmental controls. Termination policies also would mean the institution of federal and state laws on tribal lands, the closing of BIA schools, and an end to federal health services. At this point, the Navajo Nation cannot afford to provide these services to its people, and although it remains a government ward, this status has not hindered the tribe's progress. During the years that other tribes suffered as they strove for independence, the Navajo were busy setting the groundwork for a stable self-government within the confines of the reservation system.

The Organization of the Dine'

After Bosque Redondo, the Navajo still had some control over their own lives. Respected elder leaders, called *na'tanii,* made many decisions within their own small groups. Anthropologist James F. Downs describes the honor this way: "The position of the na'tanii was never formal, and no man could claim the position by virtue of inheritance or even because he had been so considered in the past. The authority of the na'tanii rested entirely on the willingness of the people to listen to his advice."[40]

The BIA usually handled major crises or those involving the whole tribe. Indian agents would step in and take whatever action they deemed appropriate, although they were unable to solve all problems alone; they often asked the *na'taniis* for guidance.

Still, these Navajo leaders could only speak for their own groups, not for all of the Dine', and the collection of varying opinions made unified decisions nearly impossible. In the early 1920s, when geologists found oil, uranium, and other valuable natural resources on the reservation, it was obvious that the Navajo needed another system of leadership. Therefore, the BIA selected three prominent Navajo leaders—Henry "Chee" Dodge, Charlie Mitchell, and Dugal Chee Bekis—as the Navajo Business Council, bestowing on them the power to make decisions about oil and uranium leases for the whole Navajo Nation.

This action did not please the Navajo people. Although the men were well respected and admired, they had been appointed by the BIA rather than chosen by the people. In 1923 the Navajo elected another council of twelve men, which allowed for equal representation for all tribe members. The delegation was named the Navajo Tribal Council, and it elected Chee Dodge to lead it as the tribal chairman (the same position is known today as the tribal president).

This was one positive step toward Navajo independence; another was the 1924 acquisition of full citizenship rights (except the right to vote, which was not granted until 1948). Yet with the privilege of citizenship also came the responsibility to America. The Navajo wanted to be good citizens, but once again heavy-handed government regulation was about to disrupt their lives.

Respected members of the tribe formed a council to decide on important matters of business regarding the oil and uranium resources on Navajo lands.

Citizenship and Harsh Responsibility

An ongoing problem of regional ecology was made worse by federal policy in the 1930s. Ever since the 1880s, BIA officials had worried that the Navajo owned more sheep than the available pastures could support. The herds ate so much that the land was being stripped of all plants and grasses. This overgrazing meant that plant roots were unable to hold water in the soil, which was washing away. This erosion created gulleys and crevasses, making the land useless. Navajo and BIA observers alike noted this deterioration in the environment.

During the twentieth century, conservationists worried about creating a dust bowl like the one that was devastating the Midwest around the same time. There, black blizzards of loose topsoil were blown through the air, blocking out the sun and creating huge drifts of dirt. The situation was so bad that many people had to leave their homes.

In 1931 the BIA finally decided to take steps to prevent the same problem from happening in the desert of the Southwest. To government officials, the problem had a simple solution: The Navajo would have to give up some of their sheep. The men who devised the so-called stock-reduction plan meant well. They intended to buy the

Silt from the Navajo lands threatened the proper function of the Hoover Dam.

sheep, not merely take them away, and they hoped that the proposal would preserve and possibly restore damaged reservation lands.

Another reason why the BIA decided to act at this time involved the newly constructed Hoover Dam, which was also the responsibility of the Department of the Interior, the BIA's parent organization. Tons of silt from the reservation had washed into the Colorado River, which is held

55

back by the dam. The accumulation of Navajoland silt put the efficiency of the dam itself in danger. Since the government had already spent four years and $49 million, the problem had to be solved.

John Collier, who was the commissioner of the Bureau of Indian Affairs, saw himself as a friend to the Native Americans. The decision to thin Navajo sheep herds had been made one year before Collier was appointed to office. Sympathizing with the tribe, Collier tried to make the loss of Navajo sheep less stressful by vowing to convince the government to extend the boundaries of the reservation. He also vowed to have schools built closer to students on the reservation, ensure that water systems were installed, and find more jobs for the Navajo people.

The Fiasco Known as Stock Reduction

Collier's intentions were good, but he made promises he could not keep. Moreover, since he did not realize the importance of sheep and horses in the Navajo way of life, he failed to understand the impact that stock reduction would have on the Navajo people. The Dine' measured wealth by the size of their herd. And they sometimes gave a child a lamb to teach the child about responsibility. But their feeling for the sheep went much deeper than this.

According to Navajo writer Roman Bitsuie,

Religious teaching explains that they [the sheep] are gifts from the Holy People that need to be cared for in re-

turn for sustenance. The people include the livestock in their thoughts and prayers for their family. The people's relationship with the animals is one of reciprocation, where the animals will provide wealth and sustenance in return for care and protection.[41]

Giving up their sheep was accepted only because the Navajo expected to reap the benefits Collier had promised in return.

The first stock-reduction roundups were voluntary. As time passed and the number of sheep to be reduced remained high, the Navajo Tribal Council voted for a mandatory reduction of 10 percent of each herd. Although the council made this arrangement in the spirit of cooperation with the government, the decision hurt small herders. Losing 10 percent of a small flock might mean giving up good breeding stock while a 10 percent loss to someone who owned many sheep might only mean the elimination of weaker animals. Also, with this limitation on herd size, no poor Navajo with a small herd would ever become a *rico*. Since the population who owned small herds was much greater than that with large herds, mandatory reduction made many people unhappy.

Those problems were only the beginning, though. When the process of reducing stock began, the BIA bought Navajo sheep and goats and took them to other parts of the country, where they were slaughtered to feed the poor. Yet over the many years that the program continued, weather and the ongoing Great Depression stepped in to make things even worse.

How the Indian Rights Association Helped the Navajo

After the Navajo returned from Bosque Redondo, the federal government was supposed to administer such programs as health, education, and welfare. In many respects, however, the Bureau of Indian Affairs (BIA) failed to protect or provide for the Native Americans. For example, traders came into the territory and made deals with Navajo people who were naive about the true value of their goods. Schools were open, but not many Navajo children attended. There was also a great need for improved health care.

In 1882 Herbert Welsh founded the Indian Rights Association (IRA) with the objective of assuring education, citizenship, and overall "civilization" of Native Americans. Although the IRA is often criticized for wanting to turn Native Americans into white people, it did use its influence to effect some positive change.

On the Navajo reservation, the IRA furnished farm implements, helped in the construction of irrigation systems, and oversaw the construction of a hospital stocked with needed medications. It also forced the BIA to control traders and to expand the reservation. In one venture, the IRA helped the Navajo to learn more about American society.

In 1893 Welsh and the Navajo agent for the BIA took a group of Navajo leaders to the Columbian Exposition, or World's Fair, in Chicago. The trip was not the first time that the Navajo had been away from the reservation, but it was a time of great wonder and delight. The Navajo were impressed with how hard the Americans worked and how well they lived. They were also surprised to see how many Americans were at the fair. After the delegation returned, school attendance for Navajo children rose dramatically.

So much livestock was being eliminated, and the economy was so poor, that sheep sold for only two dollars a head and goats for only one dollar. Transportation of the animals also became a problem in bad weather because the Navajo maintained only dirt roads, some of which became dangerous in rain and snow. Moreover, even animals meant for food had to be transported live because refrigerated trains and trucks were not yet invented.

The government paid the Navajo for their sheep, goats, and horses, but it asked that they do the slaughtering, taking as many animals as they needed. When the Dine' could not use any more meat or wool, government agents killed the rest of the animals, burying them in mass graves or leaving them in piles to rot. None of the meat or wool was used. To the Navajo, this was a terrible atrocity.

This situation, and the fact that Collier had been able to obtain approval for only a small addition to the reservation, compounded Navajo frustrations. Many confrontations arose between the Dine' and law enforcement officials when sheep, including family pets, were forcibly taken away from their owners. Bitterness, stemming from this disregard for Navajo beliefs and feelings, the harsh treatment of the animals, and the sense that they had been cheated, stays with the Navajo people to this day.

Performing Their Civic Duty

Stock reduction was another misstep along the rocky trail laid down by the federal government. Even still, the Dine' considered themselves to be patriotic U.S. citizens. When World War II broke out, Navajo people did not hesitate to sign up for active duty. At home, Navajo men and women worked in factories and on farms, picking sugar beets (used in place of cane sugar during the war). However, one special group of U.S. Marines helped in many significant battles.

The Navajo Code Talkers were a group of Navajo volunteers who devised a dictionary of over four hundred Navajo words to represent military language. They called a captain *besh-legai-nah-kih,* which means "two silver bars," the insignia a captain wears on his uniform.

The Code Talkers also devised an alphabet whereby each letter in English was represented by a Navajo word. For instance, the Navajo word *be-la-sana,* which means "apple," stood for the English letter

The American military relied on Navajo Code Talkers during World War II for communications that could not be deciphered by the Japanese.

A. In this way, a string of Navajo words could be used to spell out one word in English.

Since Navajo is a complex language that was not written down until modern times, fewer than fifty non-Navajo people could speak it. The Japanese were never able to break the codes. For this reason, the Code Talkers were in charge of communications for every major assault in the

Pacific—Guadalcanal, Iwo Jima, Tarawa, and Peleliu. An *Air Force Times* article by William Wrigg states, "According to Marine Corps high command, the Code Talkers saved thousands of American lives."[42] The U.S. Marines called the Code Talkers their secret weapon.

In fact, the Navajo code was so successful that the government kept the entire operation a secret until the 1960s, in case the military needed to use it again. The Code Talkers were finally recognized in 1989, when a statue was erected in Phoenix, Arizona, to honor the 420 men, 11 of whom

This statue, erected in 1989 in Phoenix, Arizona, honors the 420 Navajo Code Talkers who served in World War II.

Some Navajo Code Talker Words and What They Mean

English word	Navajo word pronunciation	Translation
alert	ha-ih-des-ee	alert
America	ne-he-mah	our mother
battle	da-ah-hi-dzi-tsio	battle
booby trap	dineh-ba-whoa-blehi	man trap
corps	din-neh-ih	clan
dive bomber	gini	chicken hawk
fighter plane	da-he-tih-hi	hummingbird
Germany	besh-be-cha-he	iron hat
lieutenant	besh-legai-a-lah-ih	one silver bar
major	che-chil-be-tah-ola	gold oak leaf
platoon	has-cish-nih	mud
Russia	sila-gol-chi-ih	red army
submarine	besh-lo	iron fish

were killed in action. Likewise, on September 17, 1992, a Code Talker exhibit was dedicated at the Pentagon in Arlington, Virginia, outside of Washington, D.C.

The Navajo have traveled a rocky road with the U.S. government. A chain of broken promises and a long history of ill treatment still lead the Navajo to view the BIA and the federal government with a nervous eye. Yet the Dine' remained strong, and the obstacles they overcame continued to make them stronger.

Chapter 6

Living on Dinetah

Today, life on the Navajo reservation is a mix of old and new lifestyles. Yet interest in traditional culture is blooming again, just as it nears the brink of extinction. One young Navajo man put it this way: "Our parents," he says, "they got taken away to boarding schools and they got Christianized and lost a lot of traditions. So what we wanted to do is skip that generation, go back to the elderlies, and learn about Navajo ways from them."[43] One of those ways is identification with the land. The reservation is more than a place to live; traditional Navajos feel that they and the land are one.

Still, the Navajo Nation does not really own Navajoland, and according to the Bureau of Indian Affairs (BIA), "there is no general law that permits a tribe to sell its land"[44] either. The Navajo reservation, as with all Native American reservations, is public land that is reserved only for the use of the Navajo tribe. It is held "in trust" for them by the U.S. government. Although the public may cross the reserva-tion, non-Navajo people may not live in Navajoland unless they work there.

Only 3.4 percent of Dinetah's popula-tion is non-Navajo. For the most part, these other residents are doctors and nurses, teachers, or missionaries. Some people just come to soak up the culture for short periods of time and live in motels. Permanent residents usually live in employer-provided housing since rental property is almost nonexistent. But there are other non-Navajo people who live in the middle of Dinetah on a reservation all their own. These are the members of the Hopi tribe.

The Navajo's Hopi Neighbors

Eventually, Navajoland came to surround the reservation given to the Hopi tribe. In an executive order issued by President Chester A. Arthur in 1882, he reserved land for the Hopi and "such other Indians as the Secretary of the Interior may see fit to set-tle thereon."[45] Not long after the Navajo had returned from Bosque Redondo, Navajo sheepherders followed their grazing animals onto part of this reservation, settling among the Hopi.

For more than seventy years, neither the Department of the Interior nor the Hopi tribe made any effort to remove the Navajo families from this land. In the 1950s, however, problems arose when surveyors found rich deposits of coal under this region, which is known as Black Mesa. Because the coal was highly prized for its low sulfur content (which meant it would burn cleaner and not pollute the air), experts estimated its value at around $10 billion.

An attorney encouraged the Hopi tribe to cash in on this valuable resource, and in 1958 he filed a lawsuit on behalf of the Hopi, trying to regain that part of the reservation occupied by the Navajo. It took four years for the court to finally decide that the Navajo were the "other Indians" mentioned in President Arthur's order. In addition, the Navajo had achieved squatters' rights, meaning that they had lived there so long that the property was virtually theirs. Except for a small area that reverted back to the Hopi, the court ruled that the Navajo and the Hopi had to share the land, which would then be known as the Joint Use Area (JUA).

Sharing the Land

This turn of events did not please the Hopi people at all. They were still unable to sell mineral rights to the land without Navajo approval, which would be hard to attain.

To the Navajo, Black Mesa holds great religious significance. According to Navajo elder Mamie Salt, "It is said to be the body of the Female Pollen Range [the Navajo equivalent of Mother Earth] lying there. It is there to protect the people. The Navajo people were told by the holy ones to leave it alone."[46]

So, the Hopi tribe's attorney went back to court. The Hopi demanded equal rights to the rich mineral deposits lying under the JUA, which the Navajo people occupied. They won these rights and in 1966 signed leases to Peabody Coal Company for one hundred square miles on Black Mesa. Knowing that the coal company would mine with or without their consent, the Navajo decided to sign their own deal with the coal company and to use the profits to benefit the Navajo people. An agreement was the only way for them to get their fair share of the money and jobs the mine would create.

The Hopi's attorney continued to exploit the potentially explosive elements of this situation. Eager to gain more of the coal mining pot, he hired a public relations firm to exaggerate the seriousness of the Hopi-Navajo conflict. The attorney urged Congress to partition the land once and for all to avoid further trouble. In 1974 the federal legislators passed the Navajo-Hopi Land Settlement Act, which divided 1.8 million acres equally between the tribes.

The act also ordered the Navajo to relocate to their portion of the JUA (which now became "partitioned" land) and the Hopi to theirs. At that time, more than ten thousand Navajo lived on the Hopi-partitioned land, but only about three hundred Hopi lived on the Navajo-partitioned land.

To ease the transition, the federal government helped some Navajo families with relocation in tract housing nearby. Although the idea of new homes in decent neighborhoods seemed like a good idea, many people lost these homes because they were unable to cope with the many new problems presented by life in mainstream America. It was an exact enactment of why Navajo leaders say they are not yet ready for termination. Some of the people lost their homes; others became severely depressed because their lives had been turned upside down. Many turned to alcohol and some committed suicide.

Again, officials had tried to ease the tension, but their well-meaning attempts failed. Today, the battle over the land continues, but with greater intensity and emotion.

The Navajo Nation tribal government center in Window Rock, Arizona.

Navajo Resistance

Many Navajo families have refused to move from Black Mesa, saying they do not want to suffer the same consequences as the people who were relocated. Much more importantly, they say they will not leave for religious reasons. As British writer Alexander Cockburn put it in 1996, "The most tell-tale proviso [condition] is that the Navajo must renounce any claim on sacred sites in the area and are prohibited from burying their dead on the land where they have lived for so long, a stipulation [requirement] that strikes at the very core of Navajo custom."[47] The Hopi counter such statements by observing that "the Navajo have migrated from Canada all over the US for centuries. They can practice their religion anywhere."[48]

In 1996 Congress tried to offer a solution whereby the Navajo could sign leases to remain on the land for seventy-five years. Some of the Dine' signed the leases, but others strongly opposed the arrangement because they would have to pay rent to the Hopi tribe and live under Hopi law.

Around 125 Navajo families (some 1,500 people) still refuse to leave or to sign a lease. Much livestock has been confiscated, and eviction notices have been posted announcing, "You will be given a notice to vacate if you continue to fail or refuse to relocate."[49] The BIA and Hopi officials say they are simply enforcing the law. They assure critics that no Navajo family has been relocated against its will, and three weeks' notice is given before agents remove any livestock.

The deadline for Navajo relocation stands at January 1, 2000. Currently, neither tribe shows signs of readiness to compromise. As Navajo Ben Benally explains, "This is an Indian war, and we will never stop until we have victory."[50]

Educating Navajo Children

The Navajo-Hopi land dispute is only one area in which the Navajo have shown great tenacity in the twentieth century. Mandatory education designed to "Americanize" the Navajo has been damaging to traditional Navajo culture. Recognizing that fact, the Navajo have taken on the task of educating their young people in standard subjects taught in any U.S. school as well as in the roots of Navajo tradition.

The first school on the reservation was a BIA school opened at Fort Defiance in the 1860s. Because the reservation's road system was so poor, and because people lived so far apart, the BIA ran many of its schools as boarding schools. Although some schools were set up in Navajoland, others were in places like Albuquerque and Phoenix or even as far away from Arizona as Pennsylvania and Kansas.

Navajo parents disliked the fact that BIA schools took children away from their families, who depended on them to help with farming or shepherding. Parents were even more upset that BIA teachers taught classes only in English. Speaking Navajo, even outside of the classroom, was forbidden. For these reasons, Navajo parents sometimes fought truant officers when they came to force Navajo children to attend school.

Most Navajo parents preferred mission schools such as St. Michael's, which was founded in 1902 and was run by Franciscan missionaries. Although the Catholic friars wanted Navajo children to become Christians, they did not insist on abandonment of their cultural heritage. In fact, St. Michael's became a center for Navajo cultural studies.

Other churches also opened mission schools on the reservation. Among them were the Presbyterians, who opened Ganado Mission School in 1906, and the

Evolution of the BIA Boarding School

When the Bureau of Indian Affairs (BIA) first opened boarding schools on the Navajo reservation, they were far different from the boarding schools of today. In those early times, children arrived at school knowing only their native language. The teachers did not know Native American languages, and they knew even less about Native American cultures. Therefore, Native American children spent their first weeks at school learning to speak English. Teaching methods were often harsh. Students caught speaking or singing in their native language might be told to stand in the corner or be hit on the hands with a ruler. These punishments were common in schools throughout America in those days, however, and the children of European immigrants often were treated in the same way. For the Native American students, the worst aspect of such schools was perhaps the loneliness they felt being away from their families.

Navajo families are extremely close, and parents treat their children with great warmth and gentleness. Since the children were also taken away from familiar surroundings and were forced to follow seemingly unreasonable rules and were fed foods (like cheese, beans, and sugar) that were very different from what they were used to, their unhappiness at the boarding schools is even more understandable.

Today, things have changed dramatically. Many Farms High School, for instance, is a BIA boarding school on the Navajo reservation with 450 students. It offers Native American cultural classes in addition to the standard high school curriculum, and students may take advantage of dances, field trips, athletics, and other activities that all other American high school students enjoy.

Christian Reformed Church, which opened the Rehoboth Mission School in 1903 near the town of Gallup, New Mexico.

Modern Schools

Today, the BIA still runs schools on the Navajo reservation, including day schools and boarding schools. Private contractors also run schools for the BIA. Public schools operate under the direction of the Arizona Board of Education. There are also parochial schools, run by churches of different denominations, as well as private schools. All serve Navajo children and handle students from kindergarten through the twelfth grade.

The Navajo are very concerned about higher education, too. In 1968 the Navajo Tribal Council founded the Navajo Community College (now Dine' College), the first community college to open on a Native American reservation. Originally established at Many Farms, Arizona, the main campus now rests at Tsaile, Arizona, with a branch campus at Shiprock, New Mexico. Aside from standard college curriculum, Dine' College offers much more for Navajo students. "At the Navajo community college our ancient culture permeates the curriculum. Students at the college, in addition to their secular learning, learn basketry, weaving, silversmithing, and other crafts, but they also learn how to be better individuals: people with self esteem,"[51] writes Navajo Al Durtschi in his "An Introduction to the Navajo Culture" on the World Wide Web.

This program seems to be highly successful as Dine' College graduates more Native American students than any other tribal college in the United States. The college offers a two-year associate's degree program, and some 67 percent of students who receive their associate's degree go on to complete a four-year degree. Dine' College president Dr. Tommy Louis believes that the cultural curriculum is important to the school's success. "Even the accrediting agency sees it as the beauty of our college," he says. "Navajo knowledge

How Native Americans Got Their Names

The minds of government officials boggled over the names of Native American children when they arrived at government-established boarding schools for their "Christian" educations. Many of them did not have surnames like Jones or Smith. When they did have last names, they were usually the same as their mothers' last names. From the European viewpoint, this was all wrong because, according to European tradition, children should have the same last names as their fathers. Furthermore, they called names like Crazy Horse, Flying Eagle, and Rain-in-the-Face uncouth and uncivilized.

Therefore, officials went about "doing the right thing." Once, when they asked an Apache boy his name, he replied, "Des-to-dah." They added a Christian first name of Max, and the boy became "Max Desto-

dah." Unfortunately, Destodah meant "don't know," so forever after the boy was "Max Don't-Know." But that was only one problem. They named other Native Americans for historical figures like George Washington and William Shakespeare, which allowed people to make fun of them. Others received the last name "BIA," which is the acronym for the Bureau of Indian Affairs, since they did not have a last name of their own.

Many Navajo names come from descriptions of themselves. "Yazzie" means short or small, "Tso" means big or hefty, and "Tsosie" means thin. These are all common Navajo last names. Begay is another common name among the Navajo because it means "his son." Many Navajo boys were probably given this last name because they would say they were their fathers' sons.

is just as relevant as Western knowledge in all areas of study, and Dine' is the only school fully committed to using it twenty-four hours a day."[52]

Where the Action Is

Still, modern Navajo are not all work and no play. On a weekend night, they might attend a "song and dance," where individuals and groups often compete for prizes. These events are similar to pow-wows, but, whereas a powwow may involve many different tribes, the song and dance is all-Navajo. It is connected to the Enemyway ceremony, although the Navajo song and dance is not religious, but social. "Today, the cultural aspects of the ceremony live on through song and dance contests or festivals. Participants dress in their finest traditional Navajo attire and recreate the traditional dances of their forefathers."[53] The spirit of the party remains, and there is plenty of great Navajo food to sample.

A buffalo dancer at the Zuni Pueblo State Fair in Albuquerque, New Mexico. The Navajo still maintain their culture through dances and festivals.

At home, Navajo people like to watch television. With the recent improvement of cable television on the reservation, highly populated areas receive about thirteen different channels. Navajo people in remote areas may receive more broadcasts via satellite dishes, including transmissions from major networks, some cable channels, and radio stations, too.

The Navajo Nation has its own AM radio station—KTNN—which first broadcast in 1986. The station offers country-and-western music, a Navajo favorite, and delivers Navajo news to even the most remote parts of the reservation. According to KTNN,

Because modern conveniences are still lacking in many areas of the reservation, radios, especially portable, are very important, with KTNN a necessity in every Navajo household. Every vehicle bought these days has a radio and due to the vastness of the reservation and the lack of supply sources within its borders, Navajos are constantly on the road traveling throughout the reservation and to border towns listening to their travel companion KTNN.[54]

Besides the use of radios for communicating, a few people in the far corners of Navajoland use cellular phones. Prices for cellular service are high because of the vast distances, however, and only the most powerful cell phones work.

Even traditional telephone calls can be expensive, and 70 percent of Navajo homes still lack telephone service. For this reason, Internet usage on the reservation is limited, although it is expanding. Most Internet service connections originate either from a school district (like the Chinle Unified School District at www.chinleusd.k12.az.us) or from Dine' College (http://crystal.ncc.cc.nm.us/).

The Navajo Nation also sponsors the Navajo Nation Fair, which is publicized as the largest Native American fair in the world. It takes place each year in early September in Window Rock, Arizona, which is also the capital of

Navajo Games

Rodeo is a favorite spectator and participant sport in Navajoland. Every year at the Navajo Nation Fair Rodeo, nine hundred Native American girls, boys, men, and women compete for prizes. Although that is the largest rodeo on the reservation, hundreds of other smaller ones are also held each year. In fact, the Navajo Nation holds more Native American rodeos than any other tribe. Rodeos even continue through the winter, with bull-riding competitions and jackpot team roping.

The Navajo do well in teams, too. Because they are used to closeness with their extended families as well as with their parents and siblings, the Navajo often grow up with a "family" spirit. In the sports world, this translates into "team" spirit, helping them work well together to achieve a common goal.

One of those activities is basketball. Navajo people love the game as fans and as participants, and basketball hoops are common additions to many Navajo homes. In 1998 fifteen Navajo players were honored as New Mexico High School All-Stars, and many players go on to win college scholarships. Basketball is not the only popular team sport, though. The Tuba City High School chess team captured the state championship for the years 1984, 1985, 1990, and 1991. Other team sports on the reservation include baseball, football, and soccer.

Breathtaking landscapes such as the channel south of Rainbow Bridge on Lake Powell, near the Arizona-Utah border, can still be seen on Navajo lands.

the Navajo Nation. The festival lasts five days, and more than one hundred thousand people enjoy the fun each year.

There are many other fairs in Navajoland as well. The Shiprock Navajo Fair takes place each October in Shiprock, New Mexico. In Tuba City, Arizona, the Western Navajo Fair is held in early fall, as are the Eastern Navajo Fair in Crownpoint, New Mexico, and the Central Navajo Fair in Chinle, Arizona.

The Wonder of Nature

Aside from organized activities, the Navajo Nation is a wonderland of outdoor entertainment. Along the border of Navajoland is Lake Powell, where fishing, boating, and swimming are the norm. On the reservation itself are twelve major lakes where folks can fish for trout or catfish and can even join in the fun of a trophy-fishing competition.

Mice Can Be Deadly

In 1993 two young, newly married Navajo people fell sick and died within a matter of days. Doctors were stunned. What they thought was a simple viral infection turned out to be so deadly that the couple had drowned in the serum from their own blood. That year, two dozen people in the United States became ill; eleven of them died from this terrible bug known as hantavirus.

Hantavirus is not a disease specific to the Navajo reservation, although the first fatalities happened there. It occurs most often in rural environments where deer mice are present, but it is very rare. When El Niño conditions arise, the extra moisture allows vegetation to thrive, which, in turn, causes rodent populations to increase. Deer mice, which frequent most parts of the United States, are the carriers of hantavirus. Released in the mouse's urine, this virus floats into the air on dust-borne particles, which its victims inhale.

A good rule is to wear the proper protection when cleaning in dark places where mice might be active. Immediate medical care is also important, although the treatment is not foolproof. A heart-lung bypass machine, which is usually used to provide oxygen to the blood of premature infants, is the only known antidote. It only works, however, if doctors can catch the virus early.

Hunting is another important outdoor activity on the reservation, where both small and big game (mainly deer) exist. Although hunters may track small game year-round, big game hunting usually spans a period between mid-September to December. Although the Navajo do not require tribe members to carry hunting permits, non-Navajo hunters are required to do so.

Those who want to compete against themselves have a variety of activities to pursue in Navajoland from hiking to bicycling. For those who crave competition, the Navajo Nation holds many road races each year. Especially attractive to the Navajo are the long-distance runs. This is not surprising since long-distance running is a skill for which the Navajo are famous.

So much of Dinetah is untouched by modern American conventions that people from all over the world come to the area for outdoor recreation. But not all of Navajoland is as quiet and as naturally beautiful as Canyon de Chelly or Monument Valley.

Living the American Lifestyle on Dinetah

Parts of Navajoland are very much like the rest of America. Fast-food restaurants, shopping malls, movie theaters, and supermarkets exist in Navajoland, just as they do throughout the United States. Yet the one thing that makes the Navajo people special is their culture, which is in danger of extinction. Many Navajo children cannot speak or even understand the language, and traditional religion is considered by some to be outdated. The Navajo Nation must take sufficient action to reverse the trend. Kelsey A. Begaye, the newly elected president of the Navajo Nation, uses this bit of verse to remind his people of what they must do to succeed:

We must bring back into our homes
Family, human, and spiritual values
To once again be a strong people.
The most important of which is
spiritual values.[55]

Chapter 7

An Eye Toward the Future in the Navajo Nation

The Navajo Nation has earned a respected place in modern America. In addition to its colorful artwork and crafts and rich cultural tradition, the Navajo Nation is respected for its impressive structure of self-government, the most sophisticated form of Native American government today.

Since the early days of its formation, the Navajo Tribal Council has undergone many changes to become the largest Native American legislature in the United States. In 1991 it became a three-branch government. Like the U.S. government, the Navajo government has executive, legislative, and judicial branches. The president and the vice president make up the executive branch; the speaker of the Navajo legislature and eighty-eight council delegates make up the legislative branch; and the Navajo Nation Supreme Court and district courts make up the judicial branch.

The political unit in Navajoland is the chapter, of which there are currently 110. Chapters are usually built around commu-nities, although new chapters may be formed if existing chapters exceed one thousand members. The number of chapters is not fixed. Delegates are elected by popular vote and meet at least four times a year in Window Rock, Arizona, at the tribal headquarters. Besides the delegates' responsibility to the people they represent, they also work in one of eleven tribal committees. Some of these committees are similar to ones formed in federal, state, and local governments. The Budget and Finance Committee, Education Committee, Public Safety Committee, and Ethics and Rules Committee are some examples.

The Navajo Tribal Council has been instrumental in improving life for the Dine'. In the 1950s alone, the council built chapter houses, revitalized the court system, and established the Supreme Court. It also created a college scholarship fund and the *Navajo Times,* an English-language newspaper that circulates throughout the reservation.

This organizational ability of the Navajo all stems from the time of the Navajo treaty with General William T. Sherman at Bosque Redondo. Because the U.S. government treated the Navajo people as one unified nation, they began to see themselves that way. From this stronger unified position, the Navajo people have been able to act as a nation. Attesting to that fact, a Navajo Tribal Council resolution made the official name of the Navajo people the "Navajo Nation" in 1969.

Good Ideas Turned Bad

Unfortunately, some projects approved by the Navajo Tribal Council have provided a great deal of strife for the Dine' over the years. In the Chuska Mountains, located northeast of Canyon de Chelly, the Navajo once conducted a forestry business that supported some six hundred jobs in its prime. But Navajo Forest Products Industries (NFPI) harvested so many trees in hopes of promoting more jobs and greater income for the tribe that the forest suffered horribly.

When the negative ecological impact of the logging operation was discovered, some tribal members formed an alliance called the Dine' CARE (Citizens Against Ruining Our Environment), which pointed out the problems. "We used to have ponds

The Navajo Tribal Council makes decisions that will affect all Navajo citizens.

and beavers," says Navajo Adella Begaye, wife of the late Dine' CARE founder Leroy Jackson. "We no longer hear the

Upheavals in Tribal Management

Few people are surprised these days when politicians end up in trouble. The power of their positions presents many temptations, and all human beings can be weak. These troubles also arise in the Navajo Nation.

In 1989 a well-respected tribal chairman named Peter MacDonald was placed on administrative leave from his position for taking kickbacks. This action divided the Navajo people into two factions—those for the former leader and those against him. At a rally for MacDonald, things turned ugly and two Navajo died. Prosecutors blamed MacDonald for inciting the riot. He was tried, convicted, and sentenced to fourteen years.

Since that time MacDonald has publicly apologized to the Dine', and in 1995 the tribe formally pardoned him. Still, requests for a federal pardon have been denied, although the former leader has been in poor health. A strong faction of MacDonald supporters still works toward his release.

In 1998 former Navajo Nation president Albert Hale resigned his position when accused of accepting corporate gifts and of using the tribe's credit card for personal purchases. He says he resigned because it would be too costly to fight the allegations, and he insists that he did nothing wrong. Hale's vice president, Thomas Atcitty, was also implicated in the alleged wrongdoing.

songbirds, and the medicine people can't even find all the plants they used to."[56]

Subsequent estimates by the Navajo forestry department say that it will take 160 years before foresting can resume. The Tribal Council shut down the mill in 1993, and the business closed permanently in 1995. Experts are still trying to decide how contaminated the site may be, and, if it is polluted, how extensive the contamination is.

More numerous environmental issues surround the troubled Black Mesa mines. The first trouble lies with the region itself. Rather than drilling to determine the location of coal deposits, the land is strip-mined. This process scrapes away the top layer of earth to expose the coal within, and the aftermath is devastating to the land. According to environmental author Judith Nies, "By the time the coal is extracted, the land has turned gray, all vegetation has disappeared, the air is filled with coal dust, the groundwater is contaminated with toxic runoff (sulfates particularly), and electric green ponds dot the landscape. Sheep that drink from such ponds at noon are dead by suppertime."[57]

Another problem lies in the way the coal company transports the coal to the generating stations. Black Mesa coal is processed in two locations: the Mohave Generating Station in Laughlin, Nevada, and the Navajo Generating Station in Page, Arizona. Although a private railroad carries coal to the Navajo station, the transmission process to the Mohave site is much more complicated. A coal "slurry line," which grinds the coal and mixes it with water so that the mixture can be sent through a pipeline to the station, bridges the 273-mile gap from the mine to the Mohave station. This takes 1 billion gallons of water a year. In a desert environment where water is scarce, slurrying is a costly endeavor, and the price is more than just financial. Nies states, "Groundwater levels have dropped, wells and springs have dried up, and the entire ecology of Black Mesa has changed: plants have failed to reseed and certain vegetation has died out."[58]

The third problem arising from Black Mesa coal mining comes from the generating stations, which burn the coal to create energy for many parts of the West, including Los Angeles, Las Vegas, Phoenix, and Tucson. The by-product of all of this burning is the emission of sulfur dioxide into the atmosphere. Sometimes in winter the cloud of pollution is so bad from the Navajo station that it masks the view of

Coal from Black Mesa mine is sent to the Navajo power generating station via a 273-mile underground pipeline.

the Grand Canyon. In 1998 the Environmental Protection Agency ordered the plant to reduce emissions by 90 percent.

Yet this action has proven beneficial in another way. A chemical process known as "scrubbing" washes sulfur dioxide from burning coal. The by-product of this action is sulfuric acid, which is also turned into cash when sold to industry.

Mining an Invisible Killer

Uranium mining has produced other problems that weigh heavily on the Dine' and their land. During the 1950s the Navajo Nation earned large sums of money in this enterprise because the U.S. government wanted the uranium to manufacture nuclear weapons. Nearly all of the uranium miners were Navajo. Mining operations were later discontinued when many of the miners fell sick with lung diseases and various forms of cancer from breathing in radioactive dust.

Now, the interest in uranium mining has returned to the Four Corners region. Some 1,440 acres of land have been leased to an Albuquerque company that plans to mine uranium via a different process. The proposed operation will extract the uranium ore from a layer of underground water-bearing rocks (known as an aquifer) and sell the element as fuel for nuclear power plants.

The leased land is private property that belongs mainly to Navajo residents of Crownpoint, New Mexico, which is located beyond the southeast corner of the Navajo reservation. The uranium there is supposedly one of the largest bands of untapped uranium in the United States; however, the aquifer supplies water to about ten thousand people in the Crownpoint area as well as to residents of Navajoland.

The extraction process is risky, and it has put a wedge between Navajo families who stand to make $1 million a year from this operation and those who insist that the water is much too valuable a resource to waste. Many Navajo are worried about the effects this mining will have on their people. Anna Frazier of Dine' CARE says, "As Navajo people, we are still living the nightmare of past uranium exploration on our lands. We ask that history not be repeated."[59]

Navajo Oil Profits Dwindle

Time has eroded another natural resource that produces income for the Navajo Nation: oil, which was first discovered in the 1920s. Early attempts at drilling for oil produced unsatisfactory results. Some drilling sites proved to be dry holes, and places where companies actually found oil ended up producing little. When larger pockets of oil and gas were discovered around the Four Corners area in the mid-1950s, they proved to be the source of millions of dollars in revenue each year for the tribe.

Today, revenues are dropping because the price of oil has been dropping around the world. Navajo president Kelsey A. Begaye says that the tribe is experiencing an economic depression, and unless the tribe devises new sources of revenue, "the Great Navajo Depression will become the final days of the Navajo people."[60] But Begaye will need the approval of the entire Navajo Tribal Council to fulfill plans made at the beginning of his term in office, one of which will make living in Navajoland more expensive.

President Begaye recently proposed a five-cent sales tax, a five-cent gasoline tax, and a tribal income tax. Currently, Kayenta, a city that caters to many tourists on their way to Monument Valley, is the only city on the reservation that charges a sales tax. The only taxes historically levied in Navajoland have been on non-Navajo energy companies and on the sale of cigarettes. The funds collected from the newly proposed taxes would be divided between the community where they are collected, the tribal general fund, and road maintenance. Estimations say the new taxes will provide between $70 and $100 million a year.

There is another possibility, though. Twice the Navajo have voted down propositions involving casino gambling, enter-prises from which many other Native American tribes obtain huge revenues. The Navajo culture frowns on gambling, considering it a disruption of harmony similar to drug addiction and drunkenness (the Navajo banned alcohol sales on the reservation in 1974). Fifty-five percent of the Dine', who voted against the gambling referendums, also worry that many tribe members could be attracted by the promise of winning their fortunes. "A lot of Navajo families find it hard to make a living as it is," says one Navajo woman. "The parents might gamble away the money, and it will be hard for the kids."[61]

Interior of the Indian Senate on the Navajo reservation near Window Rock, Arizona.

Planning the Dine' Future

So, if not taxes or gambling, what then? Many plans have come to the Navajo Tribal Council's table for discussion. One of them is to build a hotel near the entrance to Monument Valley. A resort hotel on the Arizona shore of Lake Powell is also in the works. Obviously, the Dine' want a piece of the tourism pie. Currently, they are only receiving 7 percent of the $550-million industry each year. A "Navajo Tourism Master Plan" will aim to create five thousand jobs for Navajo people and capture a larger share of the profits.

President Begaye also wants to use the $1 billion the Navajo Nation has tied up in investments for a new Navajo venture. He proposes to establish a First National Navajo Bank, which would have branches located throughout the reservation. In this way, Navajo investments will be kept within the tribe, and the money earned will be spent on the Navajo people; it will never leave the reservation.

Aside from creating income, the new Navajo president has other goals. Because so many Navajo homes are still without running water, he wants to look into bringing desalinized water from California to arid Nava-

joland. Desalinized water is ocean water from which the salt has been removed. Begaye's other goals include establishing a

Navajo Tribal Justice

Navajo justice often brings more into a situation than mere written laws and lawyers. One of the most influential and effective means of settling any dispute is to make the families of both the offender and the victim party to the solution.

Chief Justice Robert Yazzie says that Navajo justice is restorative and reparative. It is restorative because the injured relationships between the person responsible for the offense, the victim, and the community are restored. The reparative aspect is the process of repairing the damage. The Navajo call these combined measures *hozhooji naat'aanii*, which roughly means "peacemaking."

The Navajo do not believe that people in authority should make decisions for others. In a community of Navajo, one person is usually designated as the peacemaker because he or she has an ability to get along with everyone and can oversee the peacemaking process without forcing the issue.

Once the people involved and their families are assembled, an elder usually says a traditional prayer. Then the peacemaker permits all parties to speak. They tell not only what happened but also how they feel about what happened. There is no time limit. The peacemaker then gives a talk, rather like a sermon, drawing on stories from the Navajo creation myth to illustrate points about right and wrong, balance and imbalance. With both sides working together, a mutually acceptable solution to the problem is usually reached.

nonprofit fund, which could receive charitable contributions from wealthy Americans, and improving communications technology throughout the reservation.

Navajoland and its people have faced hard times in the recent past, but the Navajo's adaptability has seen them through difficulties even more serious. Through the Tribal Council, the new generation of progressive Navajo people will surely find ways to continually improve the quality of life on their reservation while holding onto the wisdom of their past. From prehistoric times through the new millennium and beyond, the Navajo hope to remain a people impressive in their ability to move ahead while maintaining their unique identity in a modern world.

Notes

Introduction: The People of Dinetah

1. Spirit of Beauty, "Trip Report, Day 1, South Kaibab Trailhead to Cremation Canyon." http://web2.airmail.net/zill/night.htm.

Chapter 1: Coming to Four Corners

2. James F. Downs, *The Navajo.* New York: Holt, Rinehart, and Winston, 1972, p. 7.

3. Downs, *The Navajo,* p. 7.

4. Quoted in Australian Pagan Information Centre, "Navajo Religion: A Sacred Way of Life," *Panthology,* Spring 1995. www.newage.com.au/panthology/navajo.html.

5. Matthew Jaffe, "The Gods Walk Here," *Sunset,* November 1998, p. 72.

6. Quoted in Linda Duval, "Valley a Monument to Geologic History, but Hollywood Lured by Scenery," *Gazette.* www.azcentral.com/travel/destinations/arizona/indian/monument.shtml.

7. Donald G. Pike, *Anasazi: Ancient People of the Rock.* Palo Alto, CA: American West, 1974, p. 16.

8. Pedro de Castaneda, "The Journey of Coronado," from PBS, *The West.* www.pbs.org/weta/thewest/wpages/wpgs610/corona1.htm

Chapter 2: A Picture of the Dine'

9. Bertha P. Dutton, ed., *Indians of the Southwest.* Santa Fe, NM: Southwest-ern Association on Indian Affairs, 1960, p. 32.

10. Quoted in Sue Doerfler, "B&B Gives Education in Navajo Culture," *Arizona Republic.* www.azcentral.com/travel/destinations/arizona/indian/hogan.shtml.

11. M. J. Riordan, "The Navajo Indians," *Overland Monthly,* October 1890, p. 376.

12. Quoted in Douglas Preston, *Talking to the Ground: One Family's Journey on Horseback Across the Sacred Land of the Navajo.* New York: Simon and Schuster, 1995, p. 91.

13. Quoted in Eric Volante, "Respectful Ways Go a Long Ways on Arizona Indian Lands," *Arizona Daily Star.* www.navajocentral.org/etiquette.htm.

14. Quoted in Volante, "Respectful Ways Go a Long Ways on Arizona Indian Lands."

15. Quoted in Duval, "Valley a Monument to Geologic History, but Hollywood Lured by Scenery."

Chapter 3: Navajo Spirituality

16. Quoted in Jim Lo Scalzo, "Keeping Balance," *World & I,* June 1995, p. 290.

17. Quoted in Preston, *Talking to the Ground,* p. 215.

18. Gladys A. Reichard, *Navajo Religion: A Study of Symbolism.* Princeton, NJ: Princeton University Press, 1950, p. 99.

19. Reichard, *Navajo Religion,* p. 6.

20. Reichard, *Navajo Religion,* p. 32.

21. Dutton, *Indians of the Southwest,* p. 32.

22. Indian Health Service, "Welcome to the Navajo Area of the Indian Health Service." www.ihs.gov/FacilitiesServices/AreaOffices/Navajo/gimc/Nav.asp.

23. Ron Risley, "Chinle Adventure." www.calweb.com/~risley/residency/chinle.html.

24. Quoted in Katie Monagle, "Back to the Future (Lifestyle of the Navajo)," *Scholastic Update,* February 10, 1995, p. 6+.

Chapter 4: The Long Walk and Back

25. Quoted in Preston, *Talking to the Ground,* p. 172.

26. Quoted in Alvin M. Josephy Jr., *500 Nations: An Illustrated History of North American Indians.* New York: Knopf, 1994, p. 351.

27. Quoted in Dee Brown, *Bury My Heart at Wounded Knee.* New York: Holt, Rinehart, and Winston, 1970, p. 18.

28. Quoted in U.S. Congress, Joint Special Committee to Inquire into the Conditions of the Indian Tribes, *Condition of the Indian Tribes, Report of the Joint Special Committee.* Washington, DC: Government Printing Office, 1867, p. a-115.

29. Quoted in U.S. Congress, *Condition of the Indian Tribes, Report of the Joint Special Committee,* p. a-96.

30. Quoted in U.S. Congress, *Condition of the Indian Tribes, Report of the Joint Special Committee,* p. a-116.

31. Quoted in U.S. Congress, *Condition of the Indian Tribes, Report of the Joint Special Committee,* p. a-97.

32. Quoted in Brown, *Bury My Heart at Wounded Knee,* p. 24.

33. Brown, *Bury My Heart at Wounded Knee,* p. 27.

34. Quoted in Josephy, *500 Nations,* p. 350.

35. Quoted in U.S. Congress, *Condition of the Indian Tribes, Report of the Joint Special Committee,* p. a-144.

36. Quoted in Josephy, *500 Nations,* p. 357.

37. Quoted in Josephy, *500 Nations,* p. 357.

Chapter 5: The Navajo and the U.S. Government

38. "Cherokee Nation v. Georgia," West Film Project. www.pbs.org/weta/thewest/wpages/wpgs620/cherokee.htm.

39. U.S. Department of Defense, "Native American Briefing," January 23, 1998. http://denix.cecer.army.mil/denix/Public/Native/Reports/Briefing/najan.html.

40. Downs, *The Navajo,* p. 123.

41. Roman Bitsuie, "Holy Wind and Natural Law," American Indian Heritage Foundation. www.indians.org/welker/dineway.htm.

42. William Wrigg, "Code Talkers Saved Many Marines," *Air Force Times,* April 6, 1998, p. 39.

Chapter 6: Living on Dinetah

43. Quoted in Preston, *Talking to the Ground,* p. 213.

44. Bureau of Indian Affairs, "American Indian FAQs." www.doi.gov/bia/aitoday/q_and_a.html.

45. Quoted in U.S. Court of Appeals for the Ninth Circuit, No. 90-15003, Fourth World Documentation Project. www.halcyon.com/pub/FWDP/Resolutions/Navajo-Hopi/response.txt.

46. Quoted in Klara Kelley and Harris Francis, "Places Important to the Navajo People," *American Indian Quarterly,* Spring 1993, p. 151+.

47. Alexander Cockburn, "Alexander Cockburn's America: The Navajo Indians Are Resisting Pressure to Capture Their Lands," *New Statesman,* May 9, 1997, p. 32.

48. Daniel B. Wood, "Caught in a Tangled Web of US-Indian History," *Christian Science Monitor,* January 26, 1999, p. 12+.

49. Quoted in Wood, "Caught in a Tangled Web of US-Indian History," p. 12+.

50. Quoted in Wood, "Caught in a Tangled Web of US-Indian History," p. 12+.

51. Al Durtschi, "An Introduction to the Navajo Culture," *Self Reliant People.* www.lis.ab.ca/walton/peoples/navajo/culture.html.

52. Quoted in Pamela R. Weiger, "Dine' College Folds Unique Navajo Philosophy into Its Class Curriculum," *Community College Week,* November 2, 1998, pp. 16–18.

53. American West, "Explore the Navajo Nation." www.americanwest.com/pages/navajo2.htm.

54. KTNN, homepage. www.navajoland.com/ktnn/ktnn.html.

55. Navajo Nation, "Kelsey A. Begaye, President Elect, and Dr. Taylor McKenzie, Vice-President Elect, Platform and Issues," 1998. www.navajo.org/issues.html.

Chapter 7: An Eye Toward the Future in the Navajo Nation

56. Quoted in Paul Natonabah, "After a Heavy Harvest and a Death, Navajo Forestry Realigns with Culture," *High Country News*, October 31, 1994. www.hcn.org/1994/oct31/dir/wr4.html.

57. Judith Nies, "The Black Mesa Syndrome: Indian Lands, Black Gold," *Orion,* Summer 1998. www.orionsociety.org/nies.html.

58. Nies, "The Black Mesa Syndrome."

59. Quoted in Marsha Shaiman, "US: Uranium Mining on Navajo Lands," *Race and Class,* April–June 1998, pp. 81–85.

60. Quoted in Bill Donovan, "Navajo President, New Taxes," *Arizona Republic,* February 2, 1999.

61. Quoted in Elizabeth Manning, "Navajos Say No—Then Maybe—to Casinos," *High Country News*, April 1, 1996. www.hcn.org/1996/apr01/dir/Feature_Navajos_sa.html.

Glossary

Anasazi: Ancestors of the Pueblo Indian tribes who lived in and around the Four Corners area but disappeared around A.D. 1300.

Athabascan: Navajo ancestors who lived around Lake Athabasca Canada but migrated southward beginning around the year A.D. 1000.

boarding school: A school where students live as well as study.

chant: Also called a sing; a religious ceremony of the Navajo used to cure illness or restore balance.

chindi: An evil spirit or demon associated with the dead.

clan: A person's extended family.

cradleboard: A device made from a wooden board that supports babies so that their mothers can work with free hands.

Four Corners: The point in the United States where Colorado, Utah, Arizona, and New Mexico meet.

fry bread: The staple food made from combining flour, water, salt, and baking powder and then frying the dough in hot oil.

hand tremblers: Men or women who determine the source of a person's illness or trouble.

hataalii: Also called a singer; a person trained to carry out Navajo chant ceremonies.

hogan: A traditional Navajo dwelling.

hozho: A person's balance with the universe and everything in it.

Joint Use Area: A parcel of Arizona land reserved for the use of both Hopi and Navajo people.

matriarchy: A society in which heritage is traced through the mother.

mutton: The meat of a mature sheep; traditional Navajo food.

na'tanii: A person in which a group of people place their trust; a leader.

Na-dene: An Asian tribe; ancestors of the Navajo.

naja: A central pendant of a squash blossom necklace.

overgrazing: When livestock clear the land of vegetation, resulting in erosion.

pawn: A personal possession that is left with a pawn shop or trading post as a promise to repay a loan.

peacemaker: A person who helps families to resolve disputes.

prayer stick: A Navajo sacred object.

Querechos: The name given to the Navajo by the Spaniards who first encountered them in the sixteenth century.

sandpainting: A Navajo sacred art that depicts sacred beings and is made by "drawing" with colored sand.

silversmithing: The art of making silver jewelry.

sovereignties: Political divisions that govern themselves.

Spider Woman: The figure in Navajo mythology who taught the Dine' to weave.

squatters' rights: The rights guaranteed to people living on public land for a certain length of time by the Homestead Act of 1862.

strip-mining: The act of removing a layer of topsoil in order to extract the minerals underneath.

termination: The proposed governmental policy whereby present federal support would cease and Native Americans would become wholly self-sufficient.

walk in beauty: To find *hozho;* to remain in balance with the universe and everything in it.

For Further Reading

Books

Nathan Aaseng, *Navajo Code Talkers.* New York: Walker, 1992. The story of a group of brave Navajo marines who helped the Allies win World War II.

Raymond Bial, *The Navajo.* Tarrytown, NY: Marshall Cavendish, 1998. Information and beautiful photography make up this book about the Navajo, their culture, and their religion.

Nancy Bonvillain, *The Navajos: People of the Southwest.* Brookfield, CT: Millbrook, 1995. This overview of tribal history includes information about the present-day Navajo, including steps they have taken to preserve tribal culture.

Peter Iverson, *The Navajo.* New York: Chelsea House, 1990. This is a detailed, well-written book about Navajo life and culture in the past and present.

Monty Roessel, *Kinaalda: A Navajo Girl Grows Up.* Minneapolis, MN: Lerner, 1993. This is the story of Celinda McKelvey and her coming of age ceremony as a Navajo woman.

Lenora Begay Trahand, *The Success of the Navajo Arts and Crafts Enterprise: A Retail Success Story.* New York: Walker, 1995. This history of the Navajo Arts and Crafts Enterprise includes biographical sketches of and interviews with Navajo craftspeople.

Websites

American West (www.americanwest.com/pages/navajo2.htm). Information relating to the American West and Native Americans, including history, culture, and geography.

Bureau of Indian Affairs (www.doi.gov/bia/aitoday/q_and_a.html). Includes FAQs (frequently asked questions) about Native Americans.

Indian Health Service (www.his.gov/FacilitiesServices/AreaOffices/ Navajo/gimc/Nav.asp). Information relating to health care for Native Americans.

KTNN (www.navajoland.com/ktnn/ktnn.html). The website for the radio station of the Navajo Nation.

Harrison Lapahie Jr. (www.lapahie.com/Dine_Clans.html). This personal website teems with information about Navajo life and culture.

Navajo Times (http://navajotimes.com/). The website for the newspaper of the Navajo Nation.

Works Consulted

Books

Betty Ballantine and Ian Ballantine, eds., *The Native Americans: An Illustrated History.* Atlanta: Turner, 1993. This major work includes information about all Native American tribes, including fascinating facts about their histories, cultures, and religions.

Dee Brown, *Bury My Heart at Wounded Knee.* New York: Holt, Rinehart, and Winston, 1970. This best-seller is a well-written and thorough account of the events leading up to the ruination of Native American lands and cultures in the last half of the nineteenth century.

James F. Downs, *The Navajo.* New York: Holt, Rinehart, and Winston, 1972. Anthropologist Downs looks at Navajo customs and culture in the past and present.

Bertha P. Dutton, ed., *Indians of the Southwest.* Santa Fe, NM: Southwestern Association on Indian Affairs, 1960. This complete guide to Native American tribes living in the Southwest is a bit old, but it provides fascinating information that still holds true today.

Linda B. Eaton and J. J. Brody, *Native American Art of the Southwest.* Lincolnwood, IL: Publications International, 1993. This history and explanation of Native American arts includes many illustrations.

Alvin M. Josephy Jr., *500 Nations: An Illustrated History of North American Indians.* New York: Knopf, 1994. This comprehensive volume holds information on all Native American cultures, religions, and tribal histories.

Donald G. Pike, *Anasazi: Ancient People of the Rock.* Palo Alto, CA: American West, 1974. Pike presents the history of Anasazi life in the Southwest and speculates on the reasons for the culture's disappearance.

Lawrence Clark Powell, *Arizona: A History*. New York: W. W. Norton, 1976. The author relates Arizona state history in this book, ending with the year 1975.

Douglas Preston, *Talking to the Ground: One Family's Journey on Horseback Across the Sacred Land of the Navajo*. New York: Simon and Schuster, 1995. This account of one family's trek across the Navajo Nation is led and chronicled by respected journalist Douglas Preston.

Gladys A. Reichard, *Navajo Religion: A Study of Symbolism*. Princeton, NJ: Princeton University Press, 1950. Anthropologist Reichard lived among the Navajo for many years. This is an account of her life among them, and her insights into Navajo religion.

Bryce Walker, ed., *Through Indian Eyes*. Pleasantville, NY: Reader's Digest Association, 1995. This is a wide-ranging view of Native Americans in the past and present.

Periodicals

Jennifer Barros, "Hopis, Navajos, and a Mining Company Fight over Black Mountain," *Mother Earth News*, April/May 1998.

Katharine Bartlett, "A Brief History of Navajoland," *Holbrook Tribune-News*, December 30, 1932.

Diane M. Bolz, "The Enduring Art of Navajo Weaving," *Smithsonian*, August 1994.

Alexander Cockburn, "Alexander Cockburn's America: The Navajo Indians Are Resisting Pressure to Capture Their Lands," *New Statesman*, May 9, 1997.

Dan Cray, "Navajo vs. Navajo: A Battle over Whether to Preserve Natural Resources or Develop Them," *Time*, July 27, 1998.

Bill Donovan, "Navajo President, New Taxes," *Arizona Republic*, February 2, 1999.

William M. Edwardy, "The Navajo Indians," *Harper's Weekly*, July 5, 1890.

Ian Elliot, "Ganado Primary: A School with a Difference," *Teaching PreK-8*, October 1997.

Stephen Goode, "Reservations About Indian Paternalism," *Insight on the News,* December 22, 1997.

Matthew Jaffe, "The Gods Walk Here," *Sunset,* November 1998.

Klara Kelley and Harris Francis, "Places Important to the Navajo People," *American Indian Quarterly,* Spring 1993.

Winona LaDuke, "The Dilemma of Indian Forestry," *Earth Island Journal,* Summer 1994.

William H. Lyon, "The Navajos in the American Historical Imagination, 1868–1900," *Ethnohistory,* April 1, 1998.

Katie Monagle, "Back to the Future (Lifestyle of the Navajo)," *Scholastic Update,* February 10, 1995.

M. J. Riordan, "The Navajo Indians," *Overland Monthly,* October 1890.

Michael Satchell, "The Worst Federal Agency," *U.S. News & World Report,* November 28, 1994.

Jim Lo Scalzo, "Keeping Balance," *World & I,* June 1995.

Marsha Shaiman, "US: Uranium Mining on Navajo Lands," *Race and Class,* April–June 1998.

Pamela R. Weiger, "Dine' College Folds Unique Navajo Philosophy into Its Class Curriculum," *Community College Week,* November 2, 1998.

Daniel B. Wood, "Caught in a Tangled Web of US-Indian History," *Christian Science Monitor,* January 26, 1999.

William Wrigg, "Code Talkers Saved Many Marines," *Air Force Times,* April 6, 1998.

Documents

Frank Terry, Superintendent of U.S. Boarding School for Crow Indians, Montana, *Naming the Indians,* Electronic Text Center, University of Virginia Library, March 19, 1890. http://etext.lib.virginia.edu/modeng/modeng0.browse.html.

U.S. Treaty with the Navajos, June 1, 1868, 15 Stat. L. 667, Ratified July 25, 1868. *The Dine' Family History of Harrison Lapahie Jr.* www.lapahie.com/Dine_Treaty.html.

Internet Sources

American West, "Explore the Navajo Nation." www.americanwest. com/pages/navajo2.htm.

Australian Pagan Information Centre, "Navajo Religion: A Sacred Way of Life," *Panthology,* Spring 1995. www.newage.com.au/ panthology/navajo.html.

Linda Bayless, "Navajo Weaving," *Arizona Journal.* www.azjour-nal. com/navajo_weaving.htm.

Roman Bitsuie, "Holy Wind and Natural Law," American Indian Heritage Foundation. www.indians.org/welker/dineway.htm.

Pedro de Castaneda, "The Journey of Coronado," from PBS, *The West.* www.pbs.org/weta/thewest/wpages/wpgs610/corona1.htm.

"Cherokee Nation v. Georgia," West Film Project. www.pbs.org/weta/thewest/wpages/wpgs620/cherokee.htm.

Desert USA, "Site Report: Canyon de Chelly National Monument: Survey of Archaeological Investigations." www.desertusa/ind1/ du_cdc_arc.html.

Larry DiLucchio Homepage, "FAQs About Life on the Navajo Nation and Among the Navajo People." http://ourworld.compuserve. com/homepages/larry_dilucchio/homepage.htm#travel.

Sue Doerfler, "B&B Gives Education in Navajo Culture," *Arizona Republic.* www.azcentral.com/travel/destinations/arizona/ indian/hogan.shtml.

Al Durtschi, "An Introduction to the Navajo Culture," from *Self-Reliant Peoples,* Walton Feed. www.lis.ab.ca/walton/peoples/ navajo/culture.html.

Linda Duval, "Valley a Monument to Geologic History, but Hollywood Lured by Scenery," *Gazette.* www.azcentral.com/travel/ destinations/arizona/indian/monument.shtml.

Matthew de Ferranti, "Searching for Effective Governance at the Bureau of Indian Affairs," *LBJ Journal of Public Affairs.* http://uts. cc.utexas.edu/~journal/works/deferranti.htm.

David Hoye, "Glorious Canyon Ruins a Journey into the Past," *Arizona Central.* www.azcentral.com/travel/destinations/arizona/ indian/canyondechelly.shtml.

Indian Health Service, "Welcome to the Navajo Area of the Indian

Health Service." www.ihs.gov/FacilitiesServices/AreaOffices/Navajo/gimc/Nav.asp.

Elizabeth Manning, "Navajos Say No—Then Maybe—to Casinos," *High Country News,* April 1, 1996. www.hcn.org/1996/apr01/dir/Feature_Navajos_sa.html.

Paul Natonabah, "After a Heavy Harvest and a Death, Navajo Forestry Realigns with Culture," *High Country News,* October 31, 1994. www.hcn.org/1994/oct31/dir/wr4.html.

Navajo Nation, "Kelsey A. Begaye, President Elect, and Dr. Taylor McKenzie, Vice-President Elect, Platform and Issues," 1998. www.navajo.org/issues.html.

Judith Nies, "The Black Mesa Syndrome: Indian Lands, Black Gold," *Orion,* Summer 1998. www.orionsociety.org/nies.html.

Ron Risley, "Chinle Adventure." www.calweb.com/~risley/residency/chinle.html.

Rudolph C. Ryser, "Neo-Termination and the Reagan Administration," Fourth World Documentation Project, August 4, 1982. www.halcyon.com/pub/FWDP/Americas/neo-term.txt.

U.S. Congress, Joint Special Committee to Inquire into the Conditions of the Tribes, *Condition of the Indian Tribes, Report of the Joint Special Committee.* Washington, DC: Government Printing Office, 1867. http://moa.umdl.umich.edu/cgi-bin/moa/ sgml/mos-idx?notisid=ABB3022.

U.S. Court of Appeals for the Ninth Circuit, No. 90-15003, "Navajo Families' Response to the Agreement in Principle, Concerns, Counter-Proposal, and Request for Further Mediation," in the case of *Jenny Manybeads et al. v. United States et al.,* Fourth World Documentation Project. www.halcyon.com/pub/FWDP/Resolutions/Navajo-Hopi/response.txt.

U.S. Department of Defense, "Native American Briefing," January 23, 1998. http://denix.cecer.army.mil/denix/Public/Native/Reports/Briefing/najan.html.

Eric Volante, "Respectful Ways Go a Long Ways on Arizona Indian Lands," *Arizona Daily Star.* www.navajocentral.org/etiquette. htm.

Robert Yazzie, "The Navajo Response to Crime," University of Saskatchewan, November 1997. www.usask.ca/nativelaw/jah_yazzie2.html.

Index

Picture Credits

Cover photo: Corbis
Archive Photos, 16, 18, 26, 32, 47, 55
Archive Photos/Santi Visalli Inc., 29, 77
Bureau of Ethnology, 22
Corbis, 20, 58, 73
Corbis/The Academy of Natural Sciences of Philadelphia, 44
Corbis-Bettmann, 54
Corbis/Jan Butchofsky-Houser, 59
Corbis/Macduff Everton, 15
FPG International, 36, 40, 67, 69
Library of Congress, 43
North Wind Picture Archives, 23, 27, 38, 46, 49, 63

About the Author

Patricia Cronin Marcello lives near Sarasota, Florida, with her husband and daughter. Her first short story for children, "The Mailbox Thief," was published in *Guide* magazine in 1994. Since then, she has published pieces in *Guideposts for Kids, AppleSeeds, Calliope,* and *Church Educator.* She has been an instructor for the Institute of Children's Literature since 1997.

Ms. Marcello also writes for adults and young adults. Three of her five books (*Diana: The Life of a Princess, Matt Damon,* and *Pope John Paul II*) were published by Andrews McMeel in 1998 and two more (*Jerry Garcia* and *The Titanic*) are due in 1999.